Insight Study Guide

Rosemary O'Shea

A Streetcar Named Desire

Tennessee Williams

Tennessee Williams' A Streetcar Named Desire by Rosemary O'Shea
Insight Study Guide series

First published in 2009 by
Insight Publications Pty Ltd
ABN 57 005 102 983
89 Wellington Street
St Kilda VIC 3182
Australia
Tel: +61 3 9523 0044
Fax: +61 3 9523 2044
Email: books@insightpublications.com
Website: www.insightpublications.com

This edition published 2011 in the United States of America by
Insight Publications Pty Ltd, Australia.

ISBN-13: 978-1-921088-98-8

Library of Congress Control Number: 2011931336

Cover Design by The Modern Art Production Group
Cover Illustrations by The Modern Art Production Group,
istockphoto® and House Industries
Internal Design by Sarn Potter

Printed in the United States of America by Lightning Source
10 9 8 7 6 5 4 3 2 1

contents

CHARACTER MAP

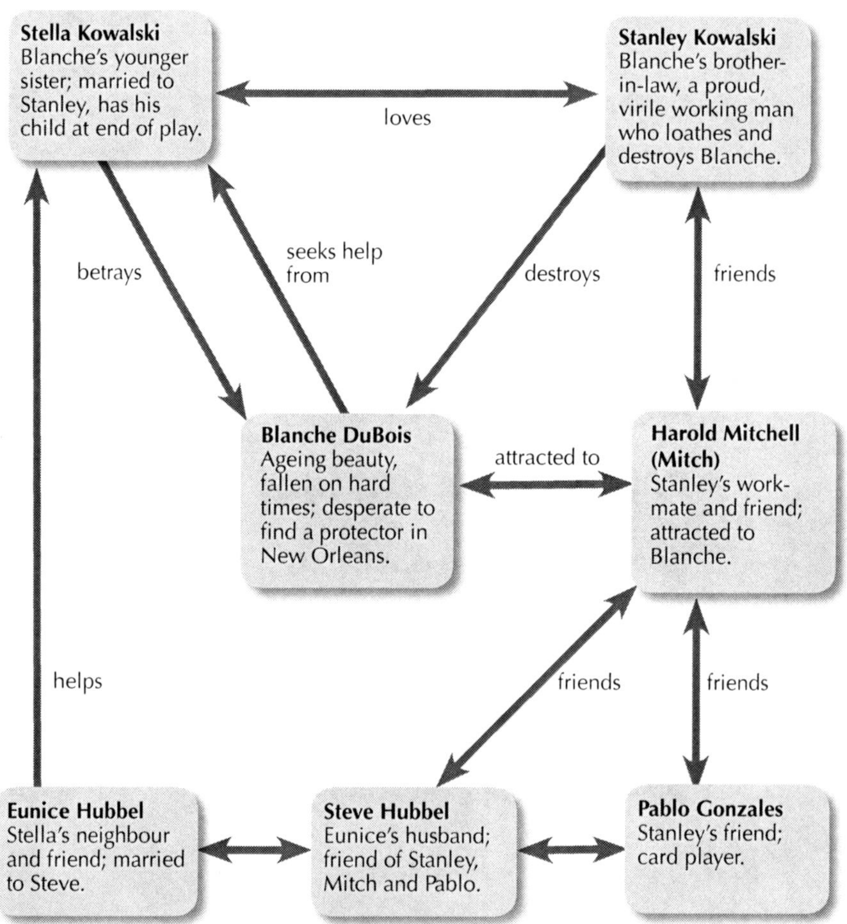

OVERVIEW

About the author

Thomas Lanier Williams was born on 26 March 1911, in Mississippi, USA. He was a shy child who endured bouts of serious illness and always suffered from the feeling of being an outsider. His family life was often unhappy. Williams' mother was a difficult woman with fantasies of being an aristocratic Southerner and his father, a travelling salesman for a shoe manufacturer, favoured Thomas' younger brother, Dakin, over the other children. His sister, Rose, suffered from mental illness and was confined to hospitals and institutions for most of her adult life.

During the 1930s Depression, Williams entered university in Missouri where his Southern accent earned him the nickname Tennessee. He could not afford to stay at university and left to take a job in a shoe factory, although he later returned to his studies, graduating from the University of Iowa.

Williams was a prolific writer of fiction, essays, poems and more than thirty plays. His earliest essays and short stories were published when he was a teenager and his first play, *Cairo, Shanghai, Bombay*, was produced in 1937, when he was at university. During World War II, *American Blues* was produced and towards the end of the war, in 1944, Williams had great success with *The Glass Menagerie*, which contains many autobiographical elements and is often thought to be his greatest work. However, it was for *A Streetcar Named Desire* that Williams received the Pulitzer Prize in 1948: a prize he later won again, in 1955 for *Cat on a Hot Tin Roof*. Williams became famous internationally in the 1950s when several of his plays, including *A Streetcar Named Desire*, were made into successful films featuring renowned Hollywood stars. Although some later works did not show the quality of his earlier writing, others, such as *Suddenly Last Summer*, *Night of the Iguana* and *Sweet Bird of Youth*, were acclaimed and also made into films.

Williams drew on his own experiences to create works that give a distinctive voice to the post–Civil War South (that is, during the late 1800s and early 1900s). The genteel but decaying society he brings to life in his plays was fast disappearing at the time during which he was writing. His plays explore sexual frustration and suppressed violence, themes that were shocking to audiences at the time. Many of his characters suffer from loneliness, often to the point of breakdown. Brutal and fragile elements counterbalance each other in many of the plays. Williams' own struggle as a homosexual man in a disapproving society; his bouts of depression; and his dependence on alcohol, barbiturates and amphetamines are reflected in the isolation suffered by the outcasts in his plays. Tennessee Williams died on 24 February 1983 at the Hotel Elysée in New York.

Synopsis

Blanche DuBois arrives at her sister Stella's home, on the edge of the French Quarter of New Orleans, hoping to stay. She is shocked by the seedy area and the shabby little apartment and has to drink several whiskies before she can face Stella, who returns from watching her husband, Stanley Kowalski, at the bowling alley. Blanche expresses dismay at Stella's poor circumstances but Stella claims to be happy and fulfilled in her marriage and way of life.

Stanley's return home unsettles Blanche, who finds him crude and vulgar. He is initially offhand about her arrival but becomes suspicious when Stella tells him that Blanche has confessed that their family home, the beautiful Belle Reve, has been lost to pay for the debts and funerals of their older relatives. Stanley accuses Blanche of trying to cheat Stella, and by extension himself, out of the inheritance. When he seizes her papers to investigate, Blanche is distressed that he has snatched some letters and poems written by her husband, who died as a young man.

Stanley is drinking and playing cards with his friends when Stella and Blanche return from an outing later that evening. Blanche is pleased by the quiet, polite Mitch, who lives with his sick mother and is a workmate of Stanley's. Stanley becomes more aggressive as he gets drunk, throwing a radio out of the window and finally hitting Stella. Blanche is horrified by his violence and takes Stella to her friend Eunice's apartment upstairs.

Stanley sobers up enough to howl in anguish for Stella outside Eunice's window. Stella comes slowly downstairs, they kiss and Stanley carries her into their home.

Blanche is appalled. The next morning she tries to convince Stella to leave and set up home with her, vowing that a rich admirer of hers will finance them. But Stella, fiercely loyal to her husband, claims that the occasional rough treatment is part of the passionate love they share. Tension grows between Stanley and Blanche, and Mitch and Blanche begin a tentative relationship. She tells him about her brief marriage, and confides that when she found that her husband was homosexual she expressed her disgust and he committed suicide. Stanley, meanwhile, has been checking up on Blanche. He has found out about her promiscuous past: her liaisons with soldiers from the local camp, her prostitution at a hotel in her home town, Laurel, and her seduction of a student – an event which led to her being virtually driven out of Laurel. Blanche is horrified to learn that Stanley has told all this to Mitch. Stanley presents Blanche with a birthday present – a one-way ticket back to Laurel – just as Stella goes into labour.

Blanche is alone in the apartment later that night when Mitch arrives, drunk and angry. Blanche asks for pity and understanding, telling him that her actions came from grief and guilt at her husband's death. He tries to rape her but stumbles out when she calls 'fire!' (p.207). She is less successful at discouraging Stanley. He returns from the hospital and turns aggressively on Blanche who has retreated into a make-believe world. Although she tries to fend him off with a broken bottle, Stanley rapes Blanche.

Several weeks later, the men are playing cards again. Stella has decided not to believe Blanche's story of the assault. To protect her marriage and the future of her child she has agreed to have her sister committed to a state mental institution. Blanche at first believes she is going on holiday and eventually responds to the doctor's gentle manner, going with him willingly. Stella is distressed and weeps, holding her baby as Stanley begins to make love to her and the play concludes.

Character summaries

Blanche DuBois

An ageing beauty, raised in a wealthy Southern family whose money has been lost. Blanche feels terrible guilt over the suicide of her young husband, Allan, and her desperation has driven her to sexual promiscuity. Forced out of her home town, she seeks a last chance at life in her sister's home in New Orleans, Louisiana. She tries to establish a relationship with Mitch, but her neurotic behaviour shows a woman on the edge of breakdown. Stanley's behaviour towards Blanche pushes her over this edge.

Stanley Kowalski

Aggressively masculine and controlling, and a proud working-class man. He despises Blanche's sense of refinement and resents her airs of superiority. He dominates Stella and is enraged when Blanche defies his authority in his own home. In the crowded little apartment, he is very aware of Blanche's sexual nature and while Stella is in hospital he takes advantage of her absence and rapes Blanche. He denies this assault to Stella and has Blanche committed as a patient at a state mental institution.

Stella Kowalski

Blanche's younger sister. She has fled the dying culture of the South where she grew up, in favour of the energy of New Orleans. Stella has married Stanley and is pregnant with their child when the play begins. Stella adores the passion and sexuality of her relationship with Stanley. Her loyalty is divided when Blanche arrives and points out his failings. Stella makes her decision at the end of the play, when she permits her sister to be committed to an institution in order to continue her own life with Stanley and their new baby.

Harold Mitchell (Mitch)

Stanley's workmate and ex–army buddy. He lives with his sick mother. He is attracted to Blanche and is ready to propose marriage until Stanley tells him about her past. Mitch becomes angry and tries to assault Blanche. Unlike Stanley, Mitch is easily confused and rebuffed. Although Blanche is ready to settle for Mitch, he is a weak, ineffectual character.

Minor characters

Eunice Hubbel, Stella's neighbour, landlady and friend. She takes Stella in when Stanley hits her.

Steve Hubbel, Eunice's husband and Stanley's friend. With Pablo, he tries to sober up the drunk Stanley by putting him under a cold shower.

Pablo Gonzales, Stanley's friend who makes up the numbers at the card table.

Negro Woman, a neighbour in this relaxed, cosmopolitan part of New Orleans. She is welcoming when Blanche arrives in Elysian Fields.

Young Man, a young man collecting for the *Evening Star* newspaper. When he comes to the apartment, Blanche, who is home alone, flatters and flirts with him, and kisses him.

Doctor and **Matron** (also called **Nurse**), staff who arrive to escort Blanche to the mental institution. While Blanche is afraid of the no-nonsense Matron, the Doctor is gallant and courteous and wins her trust.

BACKGROUND & CONTEXT

Historical and social setting

A Streetcar Named Desire was written just after World War II. The United States was emerging as a dominant global power, the world was separating into East and West along the Communist divide and the Cold War was beginning. The notion that people needed to work, to be strong and look after their own interests was growing in society, reflecting the fact that strong nations had been seen to dominate weaker ones during the war. Self-reliance and hard work were regarded as the keys to success and Stella is confident that Stanley is likely to succeed in his job because of these qualities. Stanley's forceful behaviour is an expression of this social mood, just as Blanche's clinging frailty represents weakness and failure. The postwar period was a time of change, as soldiers (like Stanley and Mitch) returned from wartime experiences in Europe and Asia, and refugees and immigrants poured into America. It was a time to question what it meant to be American.

Playwrights of the 1940s and 50s, such as Arthur Miller and Tennessee Williams, were crucial in exploring these changes to the sense of national identity. *A Streetcar Named Desire* presents the conflict between the old and the modern as Blanche's pride in her French ancestry and her cultured mind are derided by Stanley, son of Polish immigrants, who calls her 'hoity-toity' (p.199). Tensions and resentments were emerging between Americans who had been settled for generations, like the DuBois family, and the floods of immigrants who wanted to share in the country's prosperity. As industry grew and cities became bigger, rural life dwindled in importance. Great cotton plantations in the South, like Belle Reve, became impoverished and were tainted by memories of the slavery that had supported them. In *A Streetcar Named Desire*, Blanche and Stella are stranded when their wealth disappears, but while Stella embraces the new and more classless world, Blanche is unable to adapt.

When Blanche calls Stanley a 'Polack' (p.196), she demonstrates the racism that she has been brought up to accept. She is disdainful of cosmopolitan New Orleans, expecting that the Negro woman she meets in Scene One will run to fetch Stella for her. The play, however, endorses the vibrant culture of the city and the warm, easy friendships between people with different backgrounds. Racism was an even more controversial topic in America in the 1940s than it is today, and Tennessee Williams came in for some criticism from conservatives over the racial integration shown at Elysian Fields. Without explicitly naming them, the play presents issues that were unmentionable at the time, such as domestic violence and the acceptance of homosexuality. Although Stanley's possessive bullying is not really questioned by anyone but the neurotic Blanche, and Allan is referred to as a 'degenerate', Williams brought to the stage social problems that had not been dramatised before. *A Streetcar Named Desire* was seen as shocking by many people, as it broke social taboos and barriers in its presentation of modern American society.

Tennessee Williams' historical context

Williams was a Southerner, teased at university and given the nickname Tennessee for his slow Southern accent. He grew up fascinated by the history of the once glorious Southern culture, which he learned from his mother's stories. He also witnessed its decline in his lifetime. The excessive wealth of the old cotton plantations was long gone, but some of the larger-than-life characters who ran them and the genteel ladies who adorned them still lived, remnants of the past, in cities like New Orleans. Williams' plays show the progress of this decline as the decaying aristocracy was gradually overwhelmed by the energy of the rising industrial world.

Tennessee Williams was a homosexual man in a society in which homosexuality was illegal. It is not hard to see how the tensions produced by the need to present a false front to the world, and even to his mother, led to the focus on sexual behaviour and conflicts that he explores in his dramas. There are many sexual outcasts in Williams' writing. Blanche's promiscuity and Allan's suicide, when his secret is exposed, both reflect the writer's struggle to find his own place in a censorious (critical) society.

Williams was strongly influenced by writers like the English novelist D. H. Lawrence, who wrote about sexual repression and its negative impact on both men and women. Williams claimed that the major theme in all his work was the destructive effect of society on individuals who show sensitivity and are nonconformists. Those who represent conventional morality, like Stanley and Mitch, are often portrayed as intolerant and cruel. Blanche and Allan are persecuted by the righteous attitudes of conservative society and Williams elicits sympathy for sexual misfits.

There are many autobiographical elements in Williams' plays. His relationships with his family were difficult. His mother, like Blanche, was a faded Southern belle who often lamented her lost opportunities to marry well. His father, a loud, overbearing man, dismissed the boy as a weakling and may have been a model for the aggressive masculinity of Stanley Kowalski. Williams' sister, Rose, whom he loved dearly, had several breakdowns and, like Blanche, spent the last part of her life in mental hospitals.

Productions & critical reception

The first production of *A Streetcar Named Desire* opened on 3 December 1947 in New York's Barrymore Theatre. It was an instant success with New York critics, who praised the play's heightened sense of reality and uncompromising honesty. It became a blockbuster when it was filmed in 1951 and it made a star of actor Marlon Brando, who played Stanley. Tennessee Williams' plays were to have a huge impact on the development of cinema in the 1950s and 60s, and their stage productions were commercially successful throughout this period. *A Streetcar Named Desire* has also been interpreted as a ballet, and a television version was made.

However, not everyone admired Williams' work. Some critics thought that his use of symbolism and rhetoric was too flowery, with writer Mary McCarthy deciding that the play would be better named *The Struggle for the Bathroom* (Bak 2004). More widespread criticism came from those who found Williams' play immoral and shocking in its portrayal of degraded behaviour and human misery. The Legion of Decency, established by the Roman Catholic Church, found the work too sexually explicit and called for cuts to the film version, where Stella comes down the stairs to Stanley at the end of Scene Three. *A Streetcar Named Desire* played a key part in the development of a new set of social values and ideals after World War II.

Background to the story

The landowning class that Blanche belonged to depended, for its wealth and labour, on slavery. Slavery began in America in the seventeenth century and was not abolished until 1865. Black Africans were kidnapped and transported to the Southern colonies to provide free labour for large plantations growing tobacco and cotton. The rich Southerners developed their own style of genteel culture and Southern ladies became renowned for their feminine beauty and charm. However, this leisure and prosperity was propped up by the system of slavery where owners had the legal right to treat their human possessions as they wished. Much of the idea that the South was corrupt comes from the shame of this slave-owning past.

The American Civil War (1861–1865), between the Northern states and the slave-owning South, marked the end of slavery and the beginning of a slow economic decline of Southern prosperity. Although it was no longer legal to own slaves, rights for African Americans were slow to come, as the Civil Rights movement led by Martin Luther King Jr in the 1960s showed. Racism is still a potent source of social tension in the modern United States. However, in cities like New Orleans in the 1950s, where a 'melting pot' of different races maintained relative harmony (as Williams shows in his street scenes), a multicultural approach to life became widely accepted. Blanche's inability to fit into this free and easy world comes from the sense of superiority, to other races and to the poor and uneducated, that she has acquired from her Belle Reve background.

French influence began early in the history of the United States. Refugees from religious persecution in France settled in the Mississippi area from the 1600s and set up Louisiana as a French state. The Napoleonic code that Stanley describes in Scene Two still operates in Louisiana, making its legal system unique in the United States.

GENRE, STRUCTURE & LANGUAGE

Genre

A Streetcar Named Desire is a **tragedy**. It presents the downfall of the main character, Blanche, and it aims to produce a final catharsis, or emotional outlet, as we experience feelings of pity and terror at her fate. Although tragedies from ancient Greek times to Shakespeare's time were concerned with heroic characters who showed greatness and enjoyed high status, modern theatre has been more interested in the tragedies of ordinary people. *A Streetcar Named Desire* presents us with a traditionally tragic situation: a character's reversal of fortune – from a privileged, happy life into a state of misery – which can be at least partly attributed to some personal flaw or weakness.

Tennessee Williams devised the genre of the **memory play**, in which the past constantly influences the main character's present life, and he claimed that all his major plays fit this form. The memory play contains three parts. In the first part, which may have happened before the action begins on stage, a character undergoes a deeply traumatic experience. The second part is an arrest of time: a situation in which time loops back on itself so that, in the final part, the character is forced to relive the experience until its meaning becomes clear. In *A Streetcar Named Desire*, the memory play format is an effective structure to present Blanche's guilt. The traumatic experience of the first part is Allan's death. Time is arrested whenever Blanche hallucinates, hearing the Varsouviana in her mind, and the third part reveals her failure to expiate (make amends for) her past and overcome her guilt as she descends into madness.

Williams' plays also belong to the specifically American genre of **Southern Gothic**. Stories about the wealth and the decadent lifestyle of the Southern gentry and their destruction by the urban steamroller of modern American industry hold great fascination for American audiences. Blanche represents the faded, corrupt culture of the South. She is also a tragic character in a much wider sense, as her displacement and desperate loneliness are common human experiences that evoke the sympathy of any audience.

Structure

A Streetcar Named Desire presents us with two stories: the growing conflict between Blanche and Stanley, and the gradual crumbling of Blanche's sanity. The play is presented chronologically, from Blanche's arrival at Elysian Fields in May to her departure for the mental asylum in September after the long, hot summer. She is the only character who appears in every scene and this enables the audience to witness all her actions and emotions, and become privy to her secrets, such as her drinking habit. In this way, the play enables us to develop an understanding of this deeply flawed, suffering character. The chronological structure also makes us aware of Blanche's spiral into a destruction which is tragic and inevitable.

The setting of the play is limited to the Kowalskis' apartment and the street directly outside. This unity of place helps to establish the conflict between Blanche and Stanley as a fight for territorial dominance. She is an intruder in his home, bringing values and ideas that he despises and must defeat. The atmosphere of the apartment is claustrophobic and keeps the audience's attention focused on the developing conflict.

Each scene, too, has its own unity. Unlike many plays, *A Streetcar Named Desire* is not divided into acts. Instead, there are eleven scenes and each one has a similar development of conflict rising to a resolution. In Scene Two, for example, Stanley's hostility and suspicion grow as he digs into Blanche's trunk and sees her finery, but this conflict is resolved when Blanche hands over her legal papers to him. In Scene Three, Stanley is violent and abusive, but this ends with Stella forgiving him. The dramatic tension of each scene builds cumulatively, so that the final scene is a dramatic climax of all the tension that has grown throughout the passage of the play.

In every production, the director must decide when to place the intermission. Often this is set at the end of Scene Four, when Stanley has established Stella's loyalty and Blanche is at a low point. Sometimes, however, the intermission comes at the end of Scene Six, when Mitch has tentatively offered himself to Blanche, so that the second part of the production begins after her small victory. The structure of the play, then, allows some flexibility to the director in shaping the pace of the conflict.

Imagery and symbols

Music

A Streetcar Named Desire is full of music, so it is important to hear a performance of the play, as well as to read it. The music that accompanies much of the action is blues, and it expresses the free and easy nature of the neighbourhood. By contrast, the Varsouviana – a polka tune – accompanies Blanche's regression into memories of Allan's death. It begins innocently enough, striking up when Stanley first asks Blanche about her marriage, but by the end of the play the Varsouviana has become sinister, driving Blanche into a guilty panic and always ending with a gunshot.

Light

Avoiding light is important to Blanche. She covers the bare light globe with a paper shade and she refuses to meet Mitch in daylight. When he forces her to stand in the bright electric light in Scene Nine, she feels raw and exposed. Blanche is trying to avoid the physical reality of her ageing and her fading looks; her seeking shadows symbolically represents her desire to avoid facing up to her past. She tells Mitch that she loved the brilliant light of being in love with Allan but since his death the world has been dim and disappointing. Reality is now too bright and glaring for Blanche.

Bathing

Blanche is obsessed with taking baths. Her bathing is endless and represents her unsuccessful attempts to wash away her sordid past with all its cheap sexual encounters. She claims that bathing soothes her nerves but it is evident that her feeling of cleanliness never lasts long.

Names

Many of the names in *A Streetcar Named Desire* reinforce the play's central ideas. **Belle Reve**, the lost world of Blanche and Stella's childhood, is French for beautiful dream, while Stella has moved to her own earthly paradise in **Elysian Fields**. The trolley ride, the journey that Blanche takes, originates with **Desire** and ends with **Cemeteries** (p.117). **DuBois** and **Kowalski** represent clearly the different family backgrounds of the protagonists, emphasising the effete French influence and the powerful immigrant strength. Blanche tells Mitch that her first name means white (p.150), ironically suggesting a long-lost purity. When Blanche calls him **Rosenkavalier** (p.174), she is referencing a character from Richard Strauss' opera, *Der Rosenkavalier*; the name means 'knight of the rose', but the idea of the lumbering Mitch as a chivalrous, romantic hero is tragicomic in its inappropriateness.

Language

The residents of Elysian Fields speak the language of the working-class neighbourhood: earthy and direct. In contrast, Blanche emphasises her superiority by using euphemisms, calling her teaching an 'attempt to instil ... reverence' for literature (p.151). Proud of her heritage, she speaks French to show her refinement and impress Mitch. She uses the suggestive language of the temptress, calling the handsome Young Man 'honey lamb' when she is aroused by him (p.174). Although Blanche cunningly selects words to present her chosen face to the world, her poetic sensibility is genuine and reflects the sensitivity and love of beauty that are part of her character. She achieves a rhetorical flow when she is passionately putting forward a view, as she does in the 'ape' speech (pp.163–4) and when she claims the riches of the intellect in Scene Ten. However, Blanche is not always in control of her language. She slips into a vivid but sometimes incoherent stream of consciousness when she is reliving the ugly past and is lost in memories. The more distressing the memories, the more disjointed her speech becomes.

Stanley's speech represents his rough, uneducated background, but he can also speak with a heightened intensity and symbolism, as when he reminds Stella about the 'coloured lights' of their relationship (p.199). Stanley's offer to 'clear your places' (p.195) after he has broken the crockery is calculated to frighten the women. The contrast of the quiet words with the violent action shows a terrifying deliberateness and control.

A Streetcar Named Desire has no narrator to filter the story for the audience. The characters present themselves, their emotions and interactions. Williams focuses on the character of Blanche, enabling the audience to develop compassion for this troubled, unstable character, whose lies and deceptions might otherwise prove alienating. However, depending on the choices made by actors and the director, the play may present Stanley as either a cruel villain or a man fighting for what belongs to him, and Blanche as either a corrupt femme fatale or a victim of fate. The language of the play, while distinctive enough to contribute various levels of meaning to the action, is also flexible enough to allow different interpretations.

SCENE-BY-SCENE ANALYSIS

Scene One (pp.115–30)

Summary: *Blanche arrives in Elysian Fields; she tells Stella that Belle Reve is lost; Stanley and Blanche meet for the first time.*

This scene introduces Blanche as vulnerable and unhappy, and depicts the beginning of her uneasy relationship with Stanley.

Setting

Note the contrast between the relaxed poses of Eunice and the Negro Woman on the one hand, and Blanche's stiffness on the other. They are at home but she is out of place: an outsider. The street is vibrant with life but Blanche sees only poverty. The two-roomed apartment creates a problem for Blanche in its lack of privacy, and it will later become claustrophobic and seem to trap her.

Evasions

Evasiveness is one of the first characteristics Blanche displays. She is vague about her job, and under Stanley's direct questions she squirms with discomfort. It becomes clear that the subject of her marriage is painful. Her stealthy drinking shows that she needs support to get through life. Blanche's avoidance of bright light is an evasive behaviour symbolising her fear of reality.

Relationship between Stella and Blanche

The sisters love each other but long-held tensions soon emerge. Stella quietly resents her sister's bossiness and Blanche accuses Stella of deserting the family. Their characters are clearly different: Stella is trusting and readily accepts Blanche's story of losing Belle Reve; Blanche is critical and emotional, demanding attention.

Stanley makes the rules

The play foreshadows Stanley as formidable before he arrives; Stella has not told him Blanche is coming and is worried enough to warn Blanche about him. Blanche is nervous about meeting him. When he sees she has been drinking his whisky, Stanley begins to assert his rights. Stripping his shirt off is an attempt to show Blanche that she is in his territory. He enjoys her discomfort: a small cruelty. Blanche is intimidated by his power but she also registers his sexual magnetism.

Key vocabulary

Belle Reve: (French) beautiful dream.

Blue piano: sad, blues music.

Clip joint: bar or club that overcharges its customers.

Elysian Fields: Street name in New Orleans. Also the name of a heavenly paradise in Greek mythology.

Grim Reaper: traditional image of Death, dressed as a skeleton in a hooded robe.

Poe: Edgar Allan Poe, writer of horror fiction.

Por nada: (Spanish) don't mention it.

Q Think about Stanley's introduction: why is it that the first thing we see him do is throw a parcel of meat to Stella?

Q Identify all the ways in which Blanche reveals her fragility.

Scene Two (pp.131–42)

Summary: *Stanley suspects that Blanche has cheated him and Stella out of their share of Belle Reve; he ransacks Blanche's trunk; Blanche flirts with Stanley; Blanche learns that Stella is having a baby.*

In this scene, Stanley's dislike for Blanche grows, presenting itself as a mixture of distrust, resentment and contempt. Stanley and Stella argue for the first time over Blanche, marking the beginning of a change in their relationship.

Relationship between Stella and Stanley

Stanley dominates Stella although there is strong affection between them. She has to ask for money and he brushes aside her concerns about her sister. His suspicion that Blanche has cheated them is based in his possessiveness of Stella; he believes he is entitled to her property, and justifies this belief by explaining the Napoleonic code to Blanche. Stella cannot stop Stanley from rifling through Blanche's belongings. Stanley is annoyed that she has started to tell him what to do and that she calls him 'stupid and horrid' (p.134). Blanche is the unwitting catalyst for this quarrel and Stanley begins to resent the effect she is having on his docile and submissive wife.

Bloodlines

Tension is revealed over family pride. Stella defends the honesty of the DuBois family while Stanley is proud that the Kowalskis have 'different notions' (p.135). As Blanche reveals that the men of Belle Reve squandered the estate over generations, the play shows the decadence of the old culture. Their improvidence and weakness have ruined the family fortune and left her unprotected. Despite her feelings about Stanley, Blanche hopes that Stella's baby will inherit his strength and vigour and that the family can perhaps be renewed.

Illusions of wealth

Stanley has believed that Blanche was wealthy and he is genuinely suspicious about her story of losing Belle Reve. The scene shows Blanche's reduced status as Stella explains the 'feathers and furs' he drags out of her trunk (p.133). Her clothes are old, the jewellery fake and the furs a little tatty. Blanche's attempts to hide her poverty through her carefully preserved wardrobe have been exposed in her absence. Stanley will continue to expose Blanche's pretences and deceptions throughout the play.

Flirting

Because Blanche is feeling strong and relaxed after her bath, she flirts with Stanley. When she fishes for compliments, Stanley acknowledges her attractiveness but despises her need for admiration. She continues to flirt to deflect him from the topic of Belle Reve, but appears genuinely relieved to hand the legal papers over to him. Blanche seems to believe that a man should take care of business affairs and that a woman's role is to be attractive.

KEY POINT

Blanche's attempt to flirt with Stanley is unsuccessful. She is attempting to assert some control in her area of expertise – feminine attractiveness – but he sees it as a challenge to his right to dominate in his own territory. Stanley will draw on the memory of this enticement in Scene Ten and use it to justify his assault on her.

Key vocabulary

Epic fornications: numerous sexual relationships on a grand scale.

Napoleonic code: French legal system under which a husband jointly owns property his wife possesses. The state of Louisiana was formerly French territory.

Toilette: hairstyle and make-up.

Q Why does Blanche flirt with Stanley and how does he interpret her behaviour?

Q Why does Stanley give 'a bellowing laugh' (p.142) at the end of this scene?

Scene Three (pp.143–55)

Summary: *Stanley's poker night; Blanche meets Mitch and turns on the charm; Stanley hits Stella and Blanche takes her upstairs to Eunice's apartment; Stanley howls for Stella to come home and she does.*

This scene exposes the violence that Stanley uses to maintain control over others. He continues to resent Blanche's presence and the challenge she poses to his dominance.

Relationships between the men

Steve's chicken joke and the easy laughter between the men show the importance of sex in every aspect of their life. Stanley is a kind of leader, bullying the men into playing on his terms. He becomes more belligerent as he drinks more. After he hits Stella, they sober him up with a cold shower and speak to him 'quietly and lovingly' (p.152). The bond of friendship is very strong and contrasts with Blanche's isolated state.

Blanche challenges Stanley's authority

Blanche asserts her own sexual power when, half-dressed, she stares Stanley down as he enters the bedroom. She continues to play music on the radio (despite Stanley's objections) and to distract Mitch from the card game, in a calculated effort to enrage Stanley. These are brief victories for Blanche but they set Stanley even more firmly against her.

Blanche as femme fatale

Blanche finds Mitch appealing as a prospective suitor and she sets out to dazzle him with her refinement and manners. He is gullible but he rises in her esteem when he comforts her after Stanley's outburst and she genuinely begins to see Mitch as a possible sanctuary.

Domestic violence

When Stella stands up to Stanley he believes he must slap her down in order to maintain his position as ruler of the household. Several comments indicate that this is not the first time such violence has occurred. The play reflects its 1940s origins as it does not deplore the idea of domestic violence as strongly as today's audiences might. The violence takes place offstage and its impact is undercut by the fact that Stella returns to Stanley, full of forgiveness and sexual fervour.

Key vocabulary

Bobby-soxers: teenage girls wearing short socks, the contemporary fashion.
French Huguenots: Protestant refugees who settled in the Southern colonies in the seventeenth century.
Hawthorne: Nathaniel Hawthorne, American novelist.
Kibitz: to look over their shoulder at a card player's hand.
Mrs Browning: Elizabeth Barrett Browning, English poet.
Portieres: curtains covering a doorway.
Whitman: Walt Whitman, American poet.

Q Does Stella's forgiveness show that she is weak and submissive, or is it a sign of her strong relationship with Stanley?

Q What evidence is there that this is not the first time Stanley has been violent towards Stella?

Scene Four (pp.156–64)

Summary: *The morning after the poker night, Blanche rushes downstairs from the Hubbels' to rescue Stella; Blanche rages against Stanley, calling him an ape, unaware that he is listening outside; Stella greets Stanley with a fierce embrace.*

In this scene Stella chooses Stanley over her sister: a significant choice that isolates Blanche. Stanley overhears Blanche's tirade and learns of her disdain for him, and this fortifies his intention to get rid of her at any cost.

Blanche and Stella express different values about what is most important in life.

Hysteria

This scene shows Blanche's instability revealing itself under stress. Like Stella, the audience is likely to be surprised by the violence of Blanche's reaction. Blanche's vehement language, full of vivid imagery, shows her nervous imagination at work. Her frenzied movements, as she runs and throws herself on the bed and presses her hands to her lips, contrast with Stella's tranquil stillness.

Importance of sex

The play leaves us to judge whether a fulfilling sexual relationship is worth any cost, as Stella believes. Stella's languor and air of sexual satisfaction are portrayed as being more impressive than Blanche's shrill fears. Stella's view is that Stanley's occasional violence is the price of a thrilling, tumultuous marriage. Her sense of physical fulfilment is compelling and the play seems to endorse her point of view but the scene leaves a modern audience with the feeling that Stella's self-abasement lacks dignity.

Importance of culture

In a passionate speech, Blanche offers a contrasting view to Stella's. She argues that the life of the mind and spirit is what makes us human and that desire drags us down to the level of animals. The play does not fully endorse her view: Blanche's words are fervent and rousing, but her shuddering aversion to sexuality is presented as excessive.

Key Point

Stanley becomes Blanche's enemy at this point. His hostility to Blanche is hardened when he hears her describe him as 'bestial' (p.163). She has become a serious threat to his male pride. She has unwittingly strengthened his resolve to be rid of her and to destroy the sense of superiority that allows her to call him 'ape-like' (p.163). Stella's defiant embrace of Stanley is his first victory and it leaves Blanche isolated and vulnerable in the war that follows.

Key vocabulary

Bromo: a sedative.

Powder-keg: an explosive situation.

Q Is Blanche being hypocritical or truthful in this scene when she speaks so contemptuously of sexuality?

Q What words does Blanche use that show her nervous, frightened state in this scene?

Scene Five (pp.165–74)

Summary: *Stanley interrogates Blanche about the Hotel Flamingo; Blanche confesses to Stella that she has slept with many men in Laurel; Blanche tells Stella she wants to marry Mitch; Blanche flirts with the Young Man.*

This scene shows us the calculating side of Blanche as she decides to seduce Mitch into marriage. Stanley begins his campaign to undermine Blanche.

The Virgin and the Goat

These astrological signs symbolise the sexual nature of the conflict between Blanche and Stanley. Virgo signifies a chaste outlook on life, which Blanche tries to project; and the Goat, or Capricorn, symbolises lust and the will to dominate, which motivate Stanley.

Dressing up the truth

Blanche shamelessly invents ways to promote herself. The gap between the social whirl she concocts for Shep Huntleigh and the reality of the brawling neighbours is amusing. However, the gap between her past behaviour and the demure persona she is presenting to Mitch is serious. She intends to entrap him by hiding her past from him. Like Stella, the audience is torn between deploring Blanche's callous selfishness and pitying her desperation.

Vulnerability

Stanley's hint that he has begun to uncover her misbehaviour rocks Blanche. At the moment when she confesses her loneliness and fear, the audience learns Blanche has been promiscuous. This evokes sympathy for Blanche's suffering, as the scene reveals the self-destructive nature of her terror.

Reassurance

The Young Man reaffirms Blanche's confidence. She easily exerts a sexual power over him. The scene shows us that flirtation and seduction are second nature to Blanche. Despite her defence of the life of the mind in the previous scene, she is very susceptible to the attraction of a handsome stranger. Her ability to alter her persona instantly – from sexually enticing to imperious, as Mitch enters – casts doubt on her sincerity.

Key vocabulary

Daemonic: evil, devilish.
Merci: (French) thank you.
Rosenkavalier: hero of a romantic opera.
Turn the trick: pretend successfully.

Q In what ways does this scene make us question Blanche's mental stability?

Q Explain why you feel pity or contempt for Blanche in this scene.

Scene Six (pp.175–84)

Summary: *Blanche and Mitch return from a date; she is trying to lure Mitch into marriage; he tells her about his loneliness; she tells him about Allan and, moved, Mitch offers himself to her.*

Blanche is emotionally erratic in this scene, flying from depression to gaiety, from falseness to sincerity, from composure to distress in a few minutes. Although she begins by despising Mitch's impressionability, she becomes heartfelt and sincere when they discuss loss and suffering.

Teasing Mitch

Although Blanche intends to marry Mitch if she can, she mocks him in this scene. Her coy performance convinces him so easily that Blanche bursts into laughter. She takes advantage of his ignorance, inviting him in French to come to bed with her. Her expressions of admiration for him are so insincere that she rolls her eyes when he is not looking. The scene reveals her capacity for unkindness, and Mitch is also portrayed as vulnerable to this unkindness, as he appears naive and less intelligent than Blanche.

The truth hurts

Mitch's concern about losing his mother propels Blanche into honest reflection. She begins to tell Mitch about her husband but during this speech she loses touch with reality. She is lost in reliving the incident, trapped by the music in her head. Dwelling on the death of Allan is painful, and dangerous for her mental stability. From being in control a few minutes earlier, Blanche is suddenly sobbing and fearful.

A doubtful future

Although Mitch finally offers himself to her and Blanche weeps with relief, the feeling that Blanche is doomed begins to strengthen. Stanley's plans for revenge and the unfinished business of her past cast the hopeful ending of this scene in a tragic light.

Key vocabulary

Eureka: (Greek) exclamation made when something is found.
Joie de vivre: (French) liveliness, fun.
Neurasthenic: exhausted by nervous instability.
Owl-car: tram that runs late at night.
Pleiades: brilliant cluster of stars in the constellation of Taurus.
Samson: Biblical hero renowned for superhuman strength.
Voulez-vous couchez avec moi?: (French) will you come to bed with me?

Q Could Mitch and Blanche ever be happy together?

Q Which of Blanche's comments to Mitch in this scene are sincere and which are mocking?

Scene Seven (pp.185–92)

Summary: *Stanley tells Stella that Blanche has been sleeping around in Laurel; Stanley reveals that he has told Mitch the stories about Blanche; Stanley also reveals that he has bought her a bus ticket back to Laurel.*

In this scene the audience learns the full truth about Blanche while she is happily singing in the bath. The wistful lyrics, heard between Stanley's sordid revelations, evoke pity for Blanche, whose make-believe world is about to be shattered.

Stanley's moral stance

Stanley adopts a righteous attitude towards Blanche's lies. His language is lively and sarcastic, as if he is delighted to have found such rich evidence to use against her. He makes sure that Stella listens to every detail of her sister's failings. He claims to have told Mitch about Blanche out of loyalty to his old buddy. However, the extent to which Stanley relishes the details invites the audience to wonder if he is just delighted to win back the loyalty of Stella and Mitch, rather than genuinely shocked by Blanche's misbehaviour.

Stella's loyalty

Stella's defence of her sister is motivated by love. She is sickened not only by Stanley's revelations but also by the fear that they are true. She has kept Blanche's 'flighty' (p.189) character to herself and excuses Blanche many things because of the grief she suffered as a young girl. Stella fears for Blanche's future but she has already been seen to choose Stanley, and the play does not give much evidence to suggest that she will stand by Blanche now.

Blanche's longing for magic

The play uses the lyrics of a popular song to articulate Blanche's desire for love and forgiveness. Full of yearning, the words call for trust and tenderness to transform harsh reality into a kinder world. The song is a pretty, coherent expression of her need for magic; a need she tries to describe to Mitch later in the play. Blanche's singing evokes the audience's pity as we realise her cheerful mood is about to be destroyed.

Key vocabulary

Barnum and Bailey: circus owners.

Degenerate: base and degraded; used here as a euphemism for homosexual.

Flighty: unreliable, fickle.

Q Was Stanley right to warn Mitch about Blanche?

Q How do the lyrics of the song express Blanche's view of the world?

Scene Eight (pp.193–99)

Summary: *Blanche's birthday supper; Mitch does not arrive; Stanley* *becomes angry and throws crockery; Stanley gives Blanche the bus ticket back to Laurel; Stella goes into labour.*

This scene brings to a head Stanley's violent antipathy towards Blanche. His rage is directed towards both women at first, but it is Blanche whom he torments. Although he is a menacing figure at the beginning of this scene, his love for Stella is strong.

King of his home

Stanley's sudden rage at the dinner table comes from his belief that a man may act as he pleases in his own home. He asserts his territorial rights when his masculine pride is offended. He believes that Blanche has no right to put on airs of refinement. Stanley includes Stella in the abuse because she is siding with her sister. His anger passes quickly and he is much more controlled when he begins his planned torment of Blanche.

Identity

Stanley responds only mildly to the derogatory word 'Polack' (p.197) because he identifies himself as American rather than Polish. The play suggests that Blanche would not make the same claim to an American identity. Her French family origins and her devotion to European culture link her to the past, just as Stanley's immigrant background gives him the determination to make a life in the new world.

New beginnings

Ironically, Stella and Stanley's baby will come into the world on Blanche's birthday. The new baby will be 'one hundred per cent American' (p.197), as his parents are, and there will be no reminders of the lost heritage of Belle Reve in his life. The false new start Stanley offers Blanche with the bus ticket is a devastating reminder that she has nowhere to flee to, and that Elysian Fields is the end of the line for her.

Key Point

Stanley explains his motivation to Stella. He longs to be rid of Blanche so that they can resume their sexual relationship. He justifies his cruelty in the name of his marriage, but the play depicts him as having more complex motives for hating Blanche. She represents values and attitudes that challenge his masculine authority and his self esteem.

Key vocabulary

Cursed a blue streak: swore long and violently.
El pan de mais sin sal: (Mexican folk song) maize bread without salt.
Hoity-toity: conceited and haughty.
Huey Long: former Governor of Louisiana who used his power corruptly.

Q What does Stella mean when she says to Stanley that 'people like you' (p.198) caused Blanche to change?

Q What words does Stella use that show she is beginning to adopt Blanche's disrespectful attitude to Stanley? Why is she so firmly on Blanche's side in this scene?

Scene Nine (pp.200–7)

Summary: *Mitch confronts Blanche with all her lies; she admits to sleeping with the men at the Hotel Flamingo and also with the soldiers; he cannot forgive her and attempts to rape her.*

Mitch is disappointed – and disappointing

This scene reveals Mitch's limitations. His notion of a good woman is defined by the example of his mother and he is unable to find any pity for Blanche in his heart. He is not as gentle as she had hoped. His half-hearted attempt to rape Blanche, as if a fallen woman deserves nothing better, shows his conventional view of gender roles. Although this view may be typical of the time, the play presents him here as foolish and inept.

Light on the truth

As the symbolic paper shade is ripped off the lamp, Blanche is forced to face her shortcomings, and to see herself as others see her. This exposure under the spotlight prompts her into lurid revelations about her sexual past, and she portrays herself as having been a spider to her 'victims' (p.204). This wild, sarcastic image prompts the audience to reflect that the men of Laurel were equal partners in her sexual adventures, not victims, and that the censure Blanche receives is very one-sided and sexist.

Breakdown

Blanche's disjointed language shows how close she is to breakdown. She is easily distracted from Mitch and her present situation. Although heard *'barely audibly'* (p.205), the voice of the vendor is enough to send her into the past and she repeats fragments of dialogue from her memory, reliving her horror of death. The play presents her vulnerability as it provides an explanation for her promiscuous behaviour.

Key vocabulary

Boxed out of your mind: drunk.
Corones para los muertos: (Spanish) crowns for the dead.
Flores para los muertos: (Spanish) flowers for the dead.
Malarkey: nonsense, rubbish.
Uncavalier: ungallant, unlike a gentleman.

Q How convincing is Blanche's claim, 'I didn't lie in my heart'?

Q Is Mitch's view of Blanche's behaviour justified?

Scene Ten (pp.208–15)

Summary: *Stanley forces Blanche to see how pathetic she is; she threatens him with a broken bottle but he rapes her.*

Blanche's descent into madness culminates in this scene as a response to Stanley's violence. The scene brings to a head the sense of entrapment that has increased for Blanche since her arrival in the tiny apartment.

Fantasy

The story of Mitch returning with roses to apologise and beg her forgiveness is Blanche's fantasy. She turns the episode into a version of reality that she can live with: one that will not threaten her self-image. It is the dignified farewell that she would like to have achieved.

A destitute woman

Blanche clings to her idea of herself as a woman of culture and intellect, even though her disgusted look in the mirror indicates her awareness that her beauty is fading. Stanley attacks her unrealistic view of herself and forces her to recognise how tawdry her outfit is. His brutal words compel her to see herself through his eyes as a liar and a fraud. His punishment of Blanche in this scene, mental as well as physical, annihilates her.

Unequal opponents

Blanche's terror is the final catalyst for Stanley's assault in this scene. He grins at her fear and stalks her around the room. Her attempt at self-defence gives him an excuse to justify his violence but the scene still portrays him as a predator. The jungle music invites the audience to see Stanley as the 'tiger' (p.215), full of lust and power, with Blanche as his helpless victim.

Key Point

Stanley does not initially set out to rape Blanche in this scene. He is tolerant and even amused by her fantasy of an oil millionaire and invites her to drink with him. However, Blanche's praise for her own 'intelligence and breeding' (p.211) irritates Stanley. He believes she has forfeited any right to a superior attitude. Her disdain for him and for Mitch sends him into a rage and sparks the violence that follows.

Key vocabulary

Spectral: ghostly.
To bury the hatchet: to put past conflict behind.
To put on the dog: to dress up in fine clothes.

Q Stanley claims that they 'had this date with each other from the beginning' (p.215). How does Stanley justify his assault on Blanche?

Q Identify all the images of danger, in both the dialogue and the stage directions, in this scene.

Q In what ways does this scene bring to life Blanche's sense of being trapped?

Scene Eleven (pp.216–26)

Summary: *The men play poker while Stella and Eunice prepare Blanche for the mental institution; Blanche decides to trust the Doctor; Stella weeps for her sister.*

This scene shows life in Elysian Fields continuing normally, as Blanche is taken off to an institution. Stanley's callous self-interest has beaten her but Blanche shows the true style and dignity of her character as she leaves.

Luck

Stanley is jubilant in this scene. He praises his own determination to win at all costs and the play uses the game of poker, where chance and taking a gamble help to determine the outcome, to show his bold assertiveness. He sees himself as a winner.

Lies

In this scene, ironically, it is Blanche who calls for the truth, for an explanation of what has happened to her. Eunice and Stella create the fiction of a vacation with an admirer. Blanche's fantasies are used against her here, to delude her, and pity is evoked for the sick, vulnerable woman.

Dignity

Blanche achieves the dignified farewell that eluded her when Mitch left. When the Shep Huntleigh fantasy is broken, Blanche has no more stories to sustain her, and she becomes distraught. However, her decision to trust her fate to the gallantry of the Doctor is portrayed as brave and poignant.

Betrayal

This scene reveals the remorse and guilt that both Mitch and Stella feel, and in contrast Stanley appears brazen in his loud insensitivity. Stella's weeping *'with inhuman abandon'* at the end of the scene hints that perhaps Stanley's victory has not been as complete as he expected, and that his relationship with Stella will not be as easy as it was before.

Key vocabulary

Bouclé: fabric used in dresses.
Jacket: straitjacket, used to restrain violent mental patients.
Perplexity: confusion.
Pinions her arms: presses her arms against the side of her body.
Quinine: medicine which reduces fever.

Q What have Stanley and Stella learned about each other during Blanche's stay?

Q Although Blanche has lost her sanity and her hold on reality, what elements of her character remain and show through her words?

CHARACTERS & RELATIONSHIPS

Blanche DuBois

KEY QUOTES

'I won't be looked at in this merciless glare!' (Blanche, p.120)

'... I didn't lie in my heart ...' (Blanche, p.205)

'A cultivated woman, a woman of intelligence and breeding, can enrich a man's life – immeasurably!' (Blanche, p.211)

'... I have always depended on the kindness of strangers.' (Blanche, p.225)

Blanche's Southern background defines her self-image. It has taught her that beauty and charm are her greatest assets and that happiness can be found only in a relationship with a man. From the beginning, she is nervous and desperate, searching for the protection that has eluded her so far. Wracked by guilty memories, her self-image has been damaged: she is a genteel Southern lady, but she has also prostituted herself. Her desire for beauty above all has led her to regard sexuality as gross and animal, but her need for comfort has driven her into the arms of many strangers.

Blanche remains an outsider in New Orleans, openly critical of the casual life around her, which she finds vulgar. Her airs of refinement almost snare Mitch but put her in conflict with Stanley. The play enacts both her doomed search for a happy ending and her growing mental disturbance as she is forced to face the contradictions of her behaviour.

A fragile woman

Blanche has suffered many losses by the time she arrives in Elysian Fields and she is a vulnerable, isolated character. Allan's death is a trauma that has crippled her. The loss of Belle Reve is a kind of death to her as well. She has lost the protection that wealth and family standing can offer, and passionate love has brought her nothing but sorrow.

When she arrives at the Kowalskis', Blanche is desperate to find peace, security and shelter from the storm of her life. She has been seeking refuge from her guilt, which she perceives as darkness, since Allan's suicide. The sleazy Hotel Flamingo represented an illusion of shelter but it cost both her reputation and her livelihood. In New Orleans, the claustrophobic apartment provides little shelter and less privacy. Because there is nowhere else for Blanche to flee to, she sets her aim at Mitch, despite what she perceives as his blandness and mediocrity, as her last hope.

Blanche has many fears. She dreads exposure of her fading beauty under bright light almost as much as she dreads the discovery of her indiscreet past. She associates ageing with death, and her mind is full of ugly memories of death and dying. Blanche's terrors are uncontrolled as her fragile mind can cast her back to relive dreadful memories at any time.

Blanche's fractured sense of self

A key aspect of Blanche's fragile personality is that her promiscuous behaviour is at odds with the image that she wants others to see, of herself as a great lady. This contradiction destabilises her. Blanche is ambivalent about sex, seeing it as common and brutish, and yet succumbing to her desire for the young soldiers in Laurel as a release from the horrors of life at Belle Reve. After the loss of Belle Reve she descends into a double life, even more destabilising, of brief sexual encounters by night and respectable English teaching by day. Her alcoholism symbolises this damaged self-image; she is a furtive drinker, in denial about her need for drink, but dependent on it.

Blanche is proud of, and sometimes boastful about, her intellect and her cultured mind and she wants to be admired for these qualities. At the same time, flirtation, a Southern lady's greatest weapon, is ingrained in her. Blanche flirts with Stanley at first, then with Mitch and with the Young Man. It is not hard to see how dependence on male approval could lead this psychologically fragile woman to tip over the brink from flirtation to sexual promiscuity.

Key Point

Blanche's love of beauty and her sexuality combine in her response to the Young Man in Scene Five. She responds to this handsome, unexpected stranger with delight, revelling in his dazed shyness and happy to reassure herself of her attractiveness. The audience sees a glimpse of the smooth, accomplished seductress of the Hotel Flamingo. However, the positioning of this scene, just after Stanley has hinted he knows about her past and just before she turns on a practised charm for Mitch, reveals Blanche's dangerous instability.

Growing instability

Guilt has made Blanche self-destructive and her frantic search for shelter with strangers reveals how it has driven her to sexual excess. The play enacts her struggle to deny her past. She becomes ever more nervous and frightened as Stanley threatens to destroy her cover story.

Under Stanley's campaign to get rid of her, Blanche becomes progressively more unstable. Her alcohol consumption becomes more regular and the frequency of her obsessive bathing increases. Her desire to surround herself with beauty leads her to decorate the apartment with soft light, and also to portray herself falsely to Mitch. Blanche's fantasies of rescue by a wealthy admirer, Shep Huntleigh, become more real to her as she grows more frantic. Her grip on reality becomes more tenuous as reality itself becomes increasingly unbearable to her. Stanley's sexual violence is the tipping point into madness for Blanche.

Key Point

Is Blanche a victim or a predator? The play presents her lies and deceptions, her unkindness and manipulation, but it also gives her a history that goes a long way towards explaining her complexity. She has many failures and weaknesses, but Blanche is also seen to suffer greatly from the cruelty of others.

Stanley Kowalski

Key Quotes

'Stanley's the only one of his crowd that's likely to get anywhere.' (Stella, p.146)

'There's something downright – *bestial* – about him!' (Blanche, p.163)

'I'd have that on my conscience the rest of my life if I ... let my best friend get caught!' (Stanley, p.190)

'... I am the king around here, so don't forget it!' (Stanley, p.195)

'Stell, it's gonna be all right after she goes ...' (Stanley, p.195)

'We've had this date with each other from the beginning!' (Stanley to Blanche, p.215)

The play presents Stanley as the new breed of American: a tough, confident, working-class man, who will succeed in the modern world as the decayed aristocracy of the old South dies away. Swaggering and sexually assured, he has no need of the life of learning and culture that means so much to Blanche. He thrives in the vibrant, colourful world of New Orleans and feels that he can succeed at anything he tries to do.

The play pits Stanley in a struggle for dominance with Blanche, who represents all that he despises, and it slowly reveals his capacity for ruthless cruelty. The intensity of the conflict between them gives the play its dramatic tension.

Sexually motivated

Stanley's success with women *'since earliest manhood'* (p.128) has given him an air of confident masculinity. He sees women primarily in terms of their sexual attractiveness but he is not interested in coyness. His contempt for Blanche begins when she seeks compliments on her appearance. He sees flirtation as a sexual invitation, which leads him to misinterpret Blanche's teasing in Scene Two. This has its tragic consequences at the end of the play. He has convinced himself that his rape of Blanche is inevitable, that it is something she invited from the first moment of their meeting.

Masculine superiority is ingrained in Stanley's thinking. He has brought Stella down from her high social position – her 'columns' (p.199) – through sheer sexual dynamism, and their physical relationship continues to be a powerful element of the marriage. The strength of this relationship is such that Stella ignores the violence that Stanley sometimes displays when she crosses him. Blanche's claims to culture and gentility offend Stanley's belief in male superiority. He sees Blanche as corrupt and a fraud, rather than a genteel lady, and as someone who needs to be shown her lowly place.

Domineering

When he is drunk, Stanley is aggressive. The play makes it clear that he has hit Stella more than once and he is abusive to his friends over the card table after a night of drinking. The rape of Blanche is partly fuelled by alcohol, too. However, Stanley can control his behaviour when he chooses and he sometimes exerts control over others in a quieter but more ruthless way.

Stanley wants to be master in his home. His resentment of Blanche begins when she asserts her presence in the apartment, with paper lanterns and wafting perfume. More seriously, she is a rival for Stella's loyalty.

When the two women criticise his table manners, he speaks mildly but smashes crockery on the floor in a terrifying display of precisely judged violence.

Key Point

Stanley's opposition to Blanche hardens during Scene Four, when he eavesdrops on the women and hears Blanche describe him as an ape. He shows his control by smiling and greeting her when he enters the room. From this moment, he decides to do whatever he must to get rid of Blanche, to secure Stella's loyalty away from her sister and to bring Blanche down from the superior position she has adopted.

Self-interested

Although Stanley can see that Blanche is fragile, he has no sympathy for her neediness or her pretences. He actively seeks to destroy her and is cheerful when he has done so. Stella identifies his drive as ambition when she claims that he is the only one of his friends 'that's likely to get anywhere' (p.146).

Stanley insists that he is American. He identifies himself not as an immigrant 'Polack' (p.194) but as the inheritor of the new world. He is determined to take what he feels entitled to, as his insistence on the Napoleonic code shows. Stanley's 'luck' (p.216), about which he boasts in the final scene, is partly due to his ruthless self-interest. He has restored domestic peace to his home through relentless cruelty and sexual assault, and has got away with it.

Key Point

Stanley's character is open to different interpretations. Is he a man's man, contemptuous of women, who resents Blanche's air of superiority and sets out to destroy her; or is he a man who fights to preserve his home and family against a worthless, destructive intruder?

Stella Kowalski

Key Quotes

> 'The best I could do was make my own living, Blanche.' (Stella, p.126)
>
> 'But there are things that happen between a man and a woman in the dark – that sort of make everything else seem – unimportant.' (Stella, p.162)
>
> 'Oh, God, what have I done to my sister?' (Stella, p.224)

Pragmatic

Stella has changed from a DuBois to a Kowalski in more than name. Unlike Blanche, she left the dying Belle Reve to make a life for herself in the city and has abandoned the airs and graces that she would have displayed as a Southern belle. She is happy in the lively, run-down New Orleans neighbourhood, and does not show any of the longing for past grandeur that Blanche feels. Stella has settles on a life with Stanley and their child; despite Stanley's faults she is contented, until Blanche arrives to disturb their household.

Stella's pragmatism is also shown in the moral choice she makes, between Blanche and Stanley. 'I couldn't believe her story and go on living with Stanley', she tells Eunice at the end of the play (p.217). Once again, Stella decides to abandon past loyalty and to make her life in the present. It is a decision that is complicated by the arrival of the baby, and Stella understands that she has betrayed her sister.

A loving sister

The sisters' shared history means that Stella is the only character who understands Blanche and forgives her lies and her 'flighty' (p.189) behaviour. Stella's sympathy for Blanche prompts the audience to give weight to Blanche's suffering. She understands the impact of Allan's death, as she shared the life of Belle Reve at that time. Stella is a little shocked at Blanche's ruthless intention to entrap Mitch, but she sympathises with her sister's longing for refuge. Stella's role in their relationship is to reassure Blanche, and she willingly waits on her sister and tries to protect her from Stanley's cruelty.

A submissive wife

Both Stella and Blanche define themselves by their relationships with men. Blanche is shocked and amazed that Stella admits to enjoying sex too, just as Blanche herself does. Unlike her sister, though, Stella does not see this as 'brutal desire' (p.162), but as a normal part of a relationship.

Stella is thrilled by Stanley's volatility and prepared to put up with occasional violence from him. She is not downtrodden and does sometimes stand up for herself, but the play suggests that Stella's habit of submission makes it easier for her to betray Blanche at the end of the play.

Key Point

Stella's actions at the play's conclusion show how guilty and remorseful she feels. The intensity of her sobbing conveys her grief. The audience must decide whether she has betrayed Blanche out of a desire to regain her old life, or has simply submitted to her husband's wishes. She sits on the porch with the baby. We are not shown her response to Stanley's caress but it may be that her loyalty is now primarily to the child.

Mitch (Harold Mitchell)

Key Quotes

'... in all my – experience – I have never known anyone like you.' (Mitch, p.177)

'A man with a heavy build has got to be careful of what he puts on him so he don't look too clumsy.' (Mitch, p.178)

'... you seemed to be gentle – a cleft in the rock of the world that I could hide in!' (Blanche, p.205)

'You're not clean enough to bring in the house with my mother.' (Mitch, p.207)

Humble

Mitch provides a foil for Stanley. He is humble and lacking in confidence compared with Stanley's loud machismo. He is tied to his mother's apron strings, never having achieved an adult relationship of his own. This is contrasted with the aggressive sexuality which makes Stanley appear virile and dynamic. Mitch is bumbling and gullible, while Stanley is shrewd and calculating. Williams gives these two men a range of conflicting characteristics but convinces the audience of the depth of their friendship: a male bonding that has been strengthened by sharing war, work and leisure.

Genuine

Blanche sees Mitch's difference from the other men at first glance. It is his quiet politeness that registers, but also the ease with which she is able to impress him. Mitch is an easy conquest for Blanche. He is simple enough to be fooled by her pretence of virtue and is prepared to court her slowly with chaste kisses. The play presents him at first as a real possibility for Blanche: not the gallant rescuer Shep Huntleigh might be, but a genuine, warm-hearted man who admires her.

Limited

Blanche moves between amusement and gratitude in her responses to Mitch. She is prepared to settle for marriage with him as her last hope of refuge from her past, but the play makes it clear that they are unequally matched. He often fails to understand her conversation and is dumbstruck when she chatters to him in French. Mitch's response to the truth of Blanche's past shows how conventional he is. His attempt to rape her as payback for being misled indicates his conventional attitude to women: as either pure and deserving of marriage, like his mother, or ruined by their sexual appetite and deserving of ill-treatment. Mitch's remorse at the end of the play goes some way towards restoring the audience's opinion of his good heart, but he is ultimately portrayed as an ineffectual and mediocre man.

In Scene Six, Mitch is smitten with Blanche. Her false coyness impresses him mightily. Because he is so easy to convince, Blanche momentarily forgets her pretence and starts to laugh. She flatters him, pretending to admire his physique and complimenting him on his gentlemanly behaviour.

KEY POINT

Blanche's insincerity and Mitch's gullibility are so at odds in this private moment between them that the play suggests that their pairing, which both of them sincerely want, will never happen. The audience may decide, like Blanche, that he is foolish, or may feel that he is a decent man who deserves better treatment.

Steve and Eunice Hubbel

The Kowalskis' neighbours are good-hearted, working-class people who represent the neighbourhood of Elysian Fields. Eunice is pragmatic and sides with Stella in female solidarity, taking her in after the poker night. She also provides the worldly wisdom of the time, when she tells Stella to go on with her marriage despite what they both know about Stanley's treatment of Blanche. The play does not provide a critique of this view, widely held at the time, that women must ignore ugly truths in order to preserve the institution of marriage. This view is presented as sad but almost inevitable.

Steve and Eunice's marriage is conducted as a loud, public squabble: a comic contrast to the intensity of the atmosphere in the apartment downstairs. Their relationship, full of shouting and drinking, invites Blanche's disdain, but it also foreshadows Stella's fate. Having given up Belle Reve, Stella has settled for the Quarter with all its noisy abandon, and her marriage looks set to become as loud and quarrelsome as her neighbours'.

Pablo and Steve

Stanley's poker partners enjoy an easygoing, humorous friendship. They are prepared to tolerate Stanley's belligerence when he is drunk and they see him as a kind of leader; he is the captain of their bowling team and tends to call the shots when they play cards. When Stanley oversteps the social boundaries by hitting Stella, the men rush to restrain him. However, they 'speak quietly and lovingly to him' (p.152) as they put him under the cold tap, and they do not judge him for this lapse. The play makes it clear that Stanley has gone beyond acceptable moral boundaries in his treatment of Blanche when his friends comment on the way he has disposed of her. In Pablo's sad words, 'this is a very bad thing' (p.224).

Shep Huntleigh

This unseen and possibly even nonexistent character represents the protection that Blanche really longs for, and he provides a contrast with Blanche's only real suitor: the limited and conventional Mitch. Rich and generous, although inconveniently married, Shep Huntleigh, according to Blanche, shares her Southern background and knows how to appreciate a lady. He is first proposed as a rescuer when Blanche sees Stanley's violence to Stella, and he becomes increasingly real to Blanche as her hold on reality slips.

THEMES, IDEAS & VALUES

Sex and desire

KEY QUOTES

'But when the rooster catches sight of the nigger th'owing corn he ... lets the hen get away and starts pecking corn. And the old nigger says, "Lord God, I hopes I never gits *that* hongry!"' (Steve, p.144)

'But there are things that happen between a man and a woman in the dark that – sort of make everything else seem – unimportant.' (Stella, p.162)

'I seen you chasing her 'round the balcony – I'm gonna call the vice squad!' (Eunice, p.165)

'After the death of Allan – intimacies with strangers was all I seemed able to fill my empty heart with ...' (Blanche, p.205)

The driving force of sexuality is behind every point of conflict and every exchange of words in *A Streetcar Named Desire*. The very title suggests the idea of sex as a universal, irresistible force in human affairs. The setting, a crowded, noisy New Orleans neighbourhood, is filled with characters caught up in the eternal business of longing, jealousy and desire – from the sailor in Scene One to the squabbling Hubbels upstairs. Williams explores how sexual attraction, flirtation and even sexual violence underlie relationships. The play presents the idea that a person's sexual nature cannot be denied, and to attempt to deflect its course or deny its existence is to deny part of what makes us human.

A Streetcar Named Desire suggests that sexual relationships are a vital part of adult human life. People are driven to find physical satisfaction, intimacy and belonging, ideally in an exclusive partnership with another person. Those who are in such relationships fight to preserve them, like Stanley and Stella and Eunice and Steve. Those who are alone and un-partnered, such as Mitch and Blanche, reveal their loneliness and longing for the fulfilment of an intimate relationship. The central relationship, between Stella and Stanley, takes its strength from their powerful sexual bond. Stella cannot resist Stanley's anguished call to her and returns even after he has beaten her; Stanley cannot bear her leaving him and is transformed from a belligerent thug to a man weeping on his knees.

Mitch, too, is full of longing and feels strong attraction to the delicate, genteel Blanche.

Through Blanche, Williams explores the psychological danger caused when a person cannot fully accept their sexual needs as part of their own nature. This denial is part of what causes Blanche's destruction. Allan's story underlines Williams' idea: Allan is destroyed after his sad attempt to mask his homosexuality is discovered. Blanche describes the powerful desire that drives her to have sex with the young soldiers as the opposite of death; this desire was a vital life force that allowed Blanche to counter the horror of Belle Reve in its dying days.

Breaking the rules

The play provides a critique of society's hypocritical attitude to sexual behaviour. Blanche is a product of her culture, where a Southern lady's primary task is to win a wealthy husband using feminine wiles and elaborate flirtation. However, a virtuous woman must not go beyond a display of her attractions. Sex outside marriage would ruin her, by reducing her value in the marriage market. Blanche oversteps this line in her despair, and pays a price for her promiscuity. She is driven out of Laurel by the disapproval of its respectable citizens, while the men she has slept with escape censure and punishment. 'Kiefaber, Stanley, and Shaw' (p.205) appear to talk freely about their exploits at the Hotel Flamingo and show none of the shame that Blanche is made to endure. Although the social convention is that sex is permissible only within marriage, adultery by men in the Southern culture is tolerated and widespread. The DuBois 'grandfathers and father and uncles and brothers' have lost their inheritance by indulging in 'epic fornications' (p.140) over generations, unhindered by social disapproval.

The double standards, by which men and women are judged differently, are not confined to the decaying old South in *A Streetcar Named Desire*. Society turns a blind eye to the sexual misbehaviour of men in the modern world of New Orleans, too. Stanley becomes righteous when he finds out about Blanche's seamy past, and will not have her in his home. However, he rapes her and shows no remorse or guilt. Mitch, once hoping to marry Blanche, turns on her with outrage when her secrets come to light, and he, too, tries to rape her. Both men feel entitled to use sexual violence against a woman who has broken the sexual rules.

In contrast, Allan's behaviour was driven by fear of judgement. By marrying Blanche, he tried desperately to bury his homosexuality, which was seen by his society as sinful and 'degenerate' (p.190). Williams portrays Allan as a victim, a man with no future in the unforgiving society of his time.

KEY POINT

The social conventions of the time were strict for women and homosexuals. While there is sexual freedom for heterosexual men, harsh punishment is inflicted on others who break the rules. In this way, *A Streetcar Named Desire* explores patriarchal society through the prism of sex.

Domination and submission

A Streetcar Named Desire shows how sexual jealousy leads to a struggle for dominance. The play explores the idea of the couple as a primary social unit, which is threatened when a third person enters the scene. Blanche had felt betrayed and lashed out cruelly when she discovered Allan with his lover, her feelings intensified because his lover was male. The idea is given comic emphasis, too, when Eunice berates Steve for his attention to 'that blonde' (p.165).

Blanche's arrival in the Kowalskis' crowded little apartment puts stress on Stella and Stanley's relationship. Her perfume, steamy baths and paper light shades intrude into Stanley's territory. When Blanche tries to win her sister's loyalty away from Stanley, he works to destroy Blanche and keep Stella for himself. He proclaims himself a 'king' in his home (p.195), and his readiness to strike Stella and to hurl crockery show his intention to dominate.

In the context of the play, with its 1940s standards, Stella's submission to her overbearing, bullying husband appears normal. It is Blanche's hysterical reaction the morning after the poker night that is depicted as excessive. Stella, by contrast, accepts the 'rough-house' (p.215) as part of a passionate sexual relationship, just as in the end she accepts Stanley's decision to banish Blanche to the mental institution (and to certain psychological destruction) in order to save her marriage.

Blanche makes her own attempts at sexual manipulation. She flirts, with Stanley at first, then with Mitch to secure his affection, and with the newspaper collector because he is young and handsome. Stanley uses the memory of her flirtation to justify his rape of Blanche. His brute force is stronger than her efforts to win by charm. The play explores the sexual politics of power through the three main characters.

Guilt

Key Quotes

'... I've been – not so awf'ly good lately.' (Blanche, p.169)

'It was because – on the dance-floor – unable to stop myself – I'd suddenly said – "I know! I know! You disgust me ..."' (Blanche, p.184)

'Oh, God, what have I done to my sister?' (Stella, p.224)

A Streetcar Named Desire illustrates the idea that guilt can make life unendurable. Blanche cannot put her guilty memories behind her and they drive her to commit actions that ruin her future. She is haunted by guilt and forced to relive Allan's death in her memory. The play suggests that those who have strong feelings can be affected powerfully by guilt, while those who are less sensitive suffer less for their wrongdoings. Blanche's obsessive guilt may be a sign of her weakness but the play invites us to contrast her sense of moral responsibility with Stanley's thick-skinned selfishness.

Guilt without forgiveness

The play shows the corrosive power of guilt when there is no chance of forgiveness. Blanche cannot forgive herself for the outburst that led Allan to kill himself. Her cruel words were not planned but their consequence was so devastating that it caused her own psychological death. She has no chance to atone for her words or to retract them before he dies, and she remains unforgiven in her own eyes. Blanche constantly relives her trauma, tormented by the jaunty polka music. There is no sense that she has ceased to love her husband, as she speaks of him with pain and longing. It may be that guilt becomes associated in Blanche's mind with sexual indiscretion and becomes one of the factors that drives her into promiscuous behaviour, in an attempt to punish herself in some way for her attitude to Allan's homosexuality.

Guilt and punishment

Being unable to put guilt behind her, Blanche punishes herself. She cannot live fully in the present, and her mind keeps returning to the events at Moon Lake Casino, the scene of Allan's suicide. Her guilt is stronger than her will and she is weakened and destabilised by persistently dwelling on those events. She tries to numb herself with sex and alcohol against the feelings that torment her. Her constant need to bathe shows her feelings of uncleanness and Blanche is at her strongest with a drink in her hand after a long session in a hot tub.

Promiscuity without guilt

While Blanche is punished by the townspeople of Laurel for promiscuity, she does not express much shame or guilt about this, apart from admitting to Stella that she wasn't 'awf'ly good lately' (p.169). She justifies her escapades with the soldiers as a way of temporarily forgetting the horror of Belle Reve and the 'long parade to the graveyard' (p.126). She presents her promiscuity at the Hotel Flamingo as a search for shelter and, although she has to suffer social exclusion for it and it costs her Mitch's protection, it does not cause her much guilt. Stanley, by contrast, suffers no punishment for his sexual cruelty towards his vulnerable sister-in-law.

Key point

The play is more critical of conventional social morality than it is of sexual indiscretion, and suggests that cruelty is worse than sexual activity into which people enter freely.

Perceptions of guilt

The play depicts the suffering of a sensitive woman who cannot forgive herself for an action committed more than a decade ago. It also shows the insensitivity of a man without much power of introspection. Stanley shows no remorse for his rape of Blanche and in the final scene boasts about his luck – which includes getting away with sexual assault, as well as the poker game he is winning. Stanley's ruthless campaign against Blanche destroys her and he takes steps to have her committed to a mental institution, all with the single intention of removing her from the

Kowalski home. However, he feels no guilt and is concerned only about having Stella to himself. Blanche's terror of Stanley in the final scene helps audiences to pity her and to condemn his self-interest.

The play's judgement of Stanley is strengthened by the guilt that Mitch and Stella show for their part in Blanche's downfall. This guilt contrasts with Stanley's callousness; Mitch's tears and incoherent abuse evoke Stanley's contempt for such a 'bone-headed cry-baby' (p.224). Neither as hypersensitive as Blanche nor as ruthless as Stanley, Stella is forced to choose either her husband or her sister. Her choice makes her an accessory to Stanley's demolition of Blanche. She is appalled to see Blanche taken away in the custody of the state; the play leaves us with the suspicion that she will be haunted by guilt in her turn, and that Stanley's hope for things to return to what they once were will be unfulfilled.

Death and decay

Key quotes

'The long parade to the graveyard!' (Blanche, p.126)

'Why, the Grim Reaper had put up his tent on our doorstep!' (Blanche, p.127)

'And I – I'm fading now!' (Blanche, p.169)

'I – lived in a house where dying old women remembered their dead men ...' (Blanche, pp.205–6)

'Crumble and fade and – regrets – recriminations ...' (Blanche, p.206)

The play opens to *'the atmosphere of decay'* (p.115). The setting, with its *'weathered'* houses and *'rickety'* outdoor stairs (p.115), signals the transience of physical objects. The foetid warmth that is evoked suggests that things ripen and rot quickly here. The play explores the passing of youth and beauty and the end of opportunity, suggesting the inexorable and irreversible passage of time. Blanche represents a culture and way of life that is in its last days and a sense of impending destruction clings to her from the first scene.

Inevitability of death

Blanche arrives on the scene a weak, vulnerable character. Elysian Fields offers her one last chance at survival and she grabs at it desperately. Williams introduces her using the image of a moth, with its connotations of pale fragility and a brief lifespan. She is burdened with problems that threaten to overwhelm her on many occasions, and the audience witnesses her struggle to survive in a hostile environment. There is a sense of inevitability about Blanche's downfall. She is psychologically tied to her genteel past and is unable to adapt to the rough modern manners of New Orleans. Her evening gowns and tiara are incongruous in the shabby apartment and her air of superiority is misplaced. The play builds suspense as, piece by piece, the grimy past that Blanche has tried to put behind her creeps up on her. She is finally defenceless when all her 'magic' (p.204) and feminine strategies have failed and Stanley is able to annihilate her.

From the first scene, the aura of death surrounds Blanche. Her breathless stream of words to Stella in Scene One conveys the horror of physical decay: 'the struggle for breath and bleeding' (p.127) and the body that 'had to be burned like rubbish' (p.126) are memories that distress her. She has witnessed the slow death of everything she has valued, and her inability to forget makes her feel trapped. Even her struggle for life, seeking warmth with the young soldiers and protection from the men of Laurel, drags her closer to her demise. The play evokes pity for Blanche as a girl whose youth is infected by death.

Key Point

The play begins with Blanche's arrival and ends with her departure, and this gives her journey the sense of a one-way trip towards death. There is a sense of loss at the end of the play as Blanche's charm and her passionate love of beauty pass with her.

Choosing life

Those who survive have shown that they can adapt to the new world. 'The best I could do was make my own living' (p.126), Stella defends herself to her sister. Stella's defiant embrace of Stanley after the poker night and her acquiescence in having Blanche committed to the hospital show that she has left Belle Reve far behind. Her belief that Stanley will be successful and the new life resulting from their passionate sexual relationship mark Stella and Stanley out as likely to thrive. However, their survival has compromised them morally and the play leaves the audience feeling that the world they inhabit is uglier and crueller than before.

Conflicting views of reality

Key Quotes

'Blanche, I'd forgotten how excitable you are. You're making much too much fuss about this.' (Stella, p.157)

'How strange that I should be called a destitute woman!' (Blanche, p.211)

'I am not a Polack ... what I am is a one hundred percent American ...' (Stanley, p.197)

A Streetcar Named Desire presents us with protagonists who are opposed on almost every level. While Stanley is a young male at the height of his strength, Blanche is a fragile woman past her youth. She is cultured, while he is crass and sometimes cruel in his behaviour. Blanche has been raised in surroundings of wealth and privilege while Stanley, the son of immigrants, works hard to make his living. He is secure in his marriage, his friendships and his neighbourhood while Blanche, unemployed and lonely, feels acutely that she is an outsider. While she longs for love to make the world bearable, he swaggers with sexual confidence. It is hardly surprising that they interpret the world in different ways.

Stanley has no need of make-believe worlds. He is loud and confident and likes to see all the 'cards on the table' (p.137). Blanche, however, needs 'magic' (p.204) to make the world bearable, as the bright light of reality is too strong. It must not be allowed to illuminate her lurid past, her drinking problem or her fading beauty. The play enacts Blanche's descent from reality into insanity as her grip on the real world becomes weaker. Although the audience can see Blanche's failings, a strong sense of pity is evoked as the inevitability of her destruction at the hands of Stanley becomes apparent.

Different ways of seeing the world

Outlooks and values are formed from our earliest days. Blanche's world view is based on her upbringing as a member of a wealthy, landholding family where education, music and literature were valued. She is proud of her 'beauty of the mind and richness of the spirit and tenderness of the heart' (p.211) and she has a shuddering aversion to anything crude and ugly. Blanche cannot understand how Stella could have married Stanley, who is so different from the gentlemen they knew in the days of Belle Reve. She clings to the values of a way of life that is over, and she cannot find a place for herself in the raucous world of New Orleans.

Stanley, too, holds his view of the world passionately. He relies on himself and is proud of being a working-class man. While Blanche talks nostalgically of her French ancestry and her connection to European culture, Stanley is a patriotic American, living and thriving in the industrial, postwar South. He does not have much learning and feels no need for it. There is no room for pity in his world view, where only the strong survive. He is brutal in his manner and his frankness, and sees no need for subtlety or for pretence. Blanche's airs and graces at first irritate and later enrage him. The conflict caused by Stanley and Blanche's different ways of seeing life is inevitable. As Blanche struggles to reclaim Stella from *'the brutes'* (p.164), Stanley moves in to crush this rival for his wife's loyalty. Blanche's disdain for him is no match for his ruthless cruelty towards her. Stanley can see Blanche's emotional fragility but his response is to despise it as weakness.

Key point

Both characters can be seen to represent the values of their cultures and the play gives room to both world views. While the audience can appreciate Blanche's gentility and love of beauty, she represents a way of life that has decayed over generations and has almost died out by the time of the play, the mid twentieth century. While Stanley is *'common'* (p.163) and insensitive, his energy and confidence are appealing. He is a macho man who has survived war and is confident about the future. He does not hanker for anything about the past but is a man of the coming generation.

Gender-based perspectives

Blanche believes that a man's role is to protect and cherish a woman. She feels justified in flirting to show her attractiveness and to present herself in the best possible light to any admirer or prospective husband. She cannot conceive of the idea of a woman surviving independently of a man.

Key Point

The play reveals its pre-feminist origins, presenting this view as the norm, with both Stella and Eunice holding fast to their men and their marriages. Blanche describes herself coyly as an 'old maid' (p.150), a term little used today, but which in the 1940s denoted failure: a woman who could not secure a husband.

Stanley has had a great deal of sexual experience and is confident in his physical being. His love for Stella is based on a potent sexual attraction, but she is also required to be submissive and admiring. Stanley has a territorial view of his masculine rights and the play seems to question this, as Stanley is at his least attractive when he is bullying Stella. He believes that he is a 'king' (p.195) in his household, and he is intimidating and violent when he is crossed. Part of Stanley's hostility to his sister-in-law is a response to behaviour that he sees as intrusive and lacking in respect for him. Her taunts about his lack of manners, and her flirtation, which is aimed at putting him in his place, threaten his male pride.

Blanche and Stanley interpret key moments of the drama very differently. Stanley claims it is his duty to protect his buddy from the entrapment of a designing woman. Blanche sees it as part of the natural order of things that she should try to charm Mitch into marriage. Blanche turns her flirtatious charm on Stanley in Scene Two, perhaps to distract him from discussing the loss of Belle Reve, but he interprets this as an invitation to sex, which in his mind justifies the rape he commits in Scene Ten. The play throws light on the conflict that emerges when the characters interpret each other's actions from very different perspectives.

Magic or lies: hiding from the truth

Throughout the play, Blanche is portrayed as hiding from the bright light of reality. The paper light shade is a symbol of her avoidance of the glare of truth, and the wistful lyrics of 'It's Only a Paper Moon' articulate her longing to hide from a present that has become too painful to bear. 'I ... took the blows in my face and my body' (p.126), she cries to Stella in a rare moment of honesty, and it is true that her sufferings have been terrible. It is a mixture of pride and desperation that prompts Blanche to look as good as she can, to make herself and others believe she is still desirable. She knows that her looks are fading and her shrill denial of any drinking problem seems to indicate that she is aware of that, too.

Blanche, who has always been 'tender and trusting' (p.198), has had to 'make a little – temporary magic' (p.169) to find protection. However, she denies Mitch's accusation that she has lied to him. 'I didn't lie in my heart' (p.205), she tells him passionately. Even her fabrication to Stanley, that she has accepted Mitch's apology but told him their relationship is over, is not the truth but 'what *ought* to be truth' (p.204). The play invites the audience to feel pity for Blanche as her desperation seems to counterbalance her deceit. She longs for peace and refuge and we can see how this longing has driven her into risky, unwise behaviour.

The play traces Blanche's gradual descent from pretence into delusion, as her hold on reality slips. Trying to escape her past, which is full of guilt and promiscuity, she portrays herself as a woman of culture, but each of Stanley's revelations forces her to confront the ugly facts of her life. Just as he rips the paper shade off the light at the end of the play, he tears down the self-image she has tried to build. The violence of the rape is Stanley's worst blow, and it leaves her unable to distinguish between the real and the imaginary.

Key Point

Blanche is not the only character in *A Streetcar Named Desire* who takes refuge in pretence. Stella denies that there is anything wrong in her relationship with Stanley, even though she is a victim of domestic violence. Stella's decision at the end of the play, to accept Stanley's word against Blanche's, is based on pretence: we hear Eunice console her that she had no other option, and Stella chooses to believe this. In this way, the play reinforces the idea that people provide themselves with a view of life that is bearable to them.

DIFFERENT INTERPRETATIONS

Different interpretations arise from different responses to a text. Over time, a text will give rise to a wide range of responses from its readers, who may come from various social or cultural groups and live in very different places and historical periods. These responses can be published in newspapers, journals and books by critics and reviewers, or they can be expressed in discussions among readers in the media, classrooms, book groups and so on. While there is no single correct reading or interpretation of a text, it is important to understand that an interpretation is more than a personal opinion – it is the justification of a point of view on the text. To present an interpretation of the text based on your point of view you must use a logical argument and support it with relevant evidence from the text.

Critical viewpoints

Although the critics have been divided about *A Streetcar Named Desire* from the start, they have mostly agreed that the play enacts basic human conflicts, and that its concerns are not limited to its own generation and place, but relevant to people of other times and places. Some commentators have seen *A Streetcar Named Desire* as dealing with opposite types of human beings in psychological or even evolutionary terms, in which Blanche represents a dead culture and Stanley is fit to survive in the reality of the modern world.

Irwin Shaw, reviewing an early performance of the play, called it 'a despairing and lovely play' in which 'beauty is shipwrecked on the rock of the world's vulgarity'. He was most impressed by the character of Blanche, finding in her suffering an 'awesome credibility'. He welcomed the 'verselike elegance of phrase' that Williams uses, seeing in it a new turning point in American drama after the 'clipped banalities' that other playwrights had used for dialogue 'in the dreary name of realism' (Shaw 1947).

Another early critic, J. W. Krutch, reviewed the same production and found that 'the mood and atmosphere ... are almost unrelievedly morbid'. He was shocked by the 'sensational quality of the story', which in the hands of a less able writer could easily have been an 'ugly, distressing and unnecessary thing' (Krutch 1947). Both critics, however, acclaimed the play as significant and compelling.

Commentators writing in the 1940s were less likely to question the play's sexual ideology, as it presents attitudes and language that were current then, but that might be seen as sexist today. Theatre critic Rosamond Gilder described with admiration the scene in which Stella comes down to Stanley, 'drained of will, drawn by a primordial force beyond her understanding'. She claimed that this is 'a scene of masterly theatric imagination' (Gilder 1948).

Modern critics may be less comfortable with Stella's self-abasing submission to Stanley. The play's unspoken acceptance that every woman needs a man in order to complete her life, and that the right partner would have solved Blanche's problems, as she and Stella seem to believe, does not sit comfortably with a generation used to the independence that feminism has brought to women since the 1970s.

It is about the sexual ideology of the play that most interpretations have differed. Does the play present Blanche as a femme fatale who deserves and, in fact, has invited the assault by Stanley, or does it present Stanley as a ruthless destroyer who uses rape as a weapon to bring Blanche down? Some of the answer lies in the director's interpretation, and the characters have been played differently in a variety of productions. Elia Kazan, the play's first director, sympathised with Stanley, interpreting the character as a man trying to protect his home by driving off a dangerous intruder. It was reported that some audiences cheered at the rape scene in Kazan's early production.

The behaviour of the two main characters is at the heart of *A Streetcar Named Desire*, and will continue to be debated by audiences. Jo Bailey, writing about a Monash Players production, claims that 'Blanche's dishonesty about her sexuality is presented as a greater crime than Stanley's exploitation of her'. It is Blanche's inability to accept her sexual feelings as normal that underlies her conflicted ideas and outrageous behaviour. Bailey's view of the play is that Blanche must go 'because Stanley and Stella cannot have Blanche's immorality disrupting their moral order' (Bailey 1993).

Although most reviewers agree that the play is an important work of continuing relevance, some critics have been less than complimentary. Academic Robin Grove attacks the play as 'a plate of corn': shallow and obvious. He claims that the characters are so broadly drawn as to be caricatures, with Stanley as the tough guy and the women coming 'in two basic shades, "coloured" for atmosphere and white'. He attacks the constant revelations about Blanche's past as sensationalist: a game of 'How Far Can You Go'. It is not enough for her to be an alcoholic, a liar and a nymphomaniac. Grove claims that the final horror, that Blanche was married to a homosexual, is about the limit of a 1940s audience's tolerance.

Grove believes that the 'tawdry' sexual ideology of the play is distasteful and that the audience is manipulated to endorse it. Blanche 'is made to grate on our nerves by Williams' so that 'in scene 10, the real unspoken meaning of the play is that she really has been asking for what she gets'. His final criticism of the text is that it is 'as artily dolled-up – and as empty, ultimately – as the half-despised, half-identified-with heroine herself' (Grove 1987).

All the interpretations of the text hinge on a reading of the relationships between the main characters. Because of the fluid nature of a play, in which actors, a director's guidance and a stage setting may intervene between the script and our response, it is crucial to pay close attention to the written words of the text in order to develop a well-substantiated view of the play.

Two interpretations

Reading 1

***A Streetcar Named Desire* is a dramatic presentation of the inevitable survival of the fittest.**

Natural selection means, according to Darwin's theory, that those who cannot adapt to a changing environment will die out. This statement suggests that because she is so wounded and vulnerable, Blanche's fate is inevitable from the beginning of the play. As Stanley's star rises, Blanche's time is ending.

The statement suggests that Blanche is unfit to adapt to the changing world. There is much evidence for this. Her contempt for the cosmopolitan world of New Orleans shows her belief that the old ways are better and that she cannot relinquish them. Her shabby finery, delicate manners and disapproval of her surroundings all mark her as out of tune with this society. Her pretences and the comfort she seeks in alcohol show her inability to face the problems of surviving in the world as it now is.

The statement also portrays Blanche as the representative of a dying culture. The world that dies with Blanche is seen to be rotten. She reminisces about the gentility of Belle Reve, where the top strata of society had a 'coloured girl' (p.206) to change the pillow slips. This is a lingering echo of the system of slavery that the Old South was based on. Blanche still expects to be waited on, even if it is by her own sister, and this is an outdated attitude in a more egalitarian world. The men she knew in her youth, with whom she compares Stanley so unfavourably, came from a corrupt tradition of 'epic' (p.140) fornicators. The heirs of generations of wealth have squandered the DuBois inheritance and died out, leaving Blanche the last of her line as Stella has become a Kowalski survivor. Blanche's fading beauty represents the loss of all the fine, rich aspects of the culture and family that are dying out.

Stanley, by contrast, is a man of the future, fit to survive. He is a worker, not a worthless landowner with the taint of decadent slave-owning about him. He is decorated in war and lucky in cards. The play shows him as virile, a '*gaudy seed-bearer*' (p.128) new to fatherhood and with prospects in his employment. Stanley is a winner: ruthless, shrewd, demanding to get his own way and capable of using force if necessary. His vigour comes from his immigrant energy and his confidence. He is fully at home, whether in his bowling team, enjoying neighbourhood friendships or surrounded by admiring family and friends. This is his place and time.

It is inevitable that Stanley should be the agent of Blanche's destruction. She steals his liquor, criticises his manners, calls him 'ape-like' (p.163), teases him, threatens his hold over his wife and best friend and, unforgivably, thinks she is better than he is. The intolerance that Stanley feels for Blanche is the impatience of the new generation for the tiresome, outdated older generation. Stanley managed to pull Stella 'off them columns' (p.199) and he aims to bring Blanche down, too, into the real world where she will be unfit to survive.

Stella represents the adaptation that ensures survival. She has moved on, fleeing the Old South for the new, urban life of New Orleans. She has found life, sexual fulfilment, procreation and shelter – all the means of survival – in Stanley. Stella seems to have put Belle Reve behind her without a qualm. She recognises that a dying culture has nothing to offer her.

Finally, we may deplore the ruthless, machine-like destruction that Stanley unleashes, but the play suggests that there can be no other outcome. Blanche is doomed from the beginning and her world goes with her.

Reading 2

***A Streetcar Named Desire* presents Blanche as the victim of a cruel society.**

Another way of interpreting the text is to see Blanche as deliberately persecuted, rather than as an inevitable victim of a changing world. The statement above suggests that despite her courage and intelligence, Blanche is no match for the conventional morality of the time, of which Stanley is the agent. She is a victim of a hypocritical and moralistic society, one which seeks to destroy those who do not conform. She finds the world to be a 'rock' (p.205) and divides humanity into 'soft people' and 'hard ones' (p.169). All her skills and strategies backfire as she enters into relationships which today might be less remarkable, but were unacceptable for a woman in the 1940s. The spite and malice of others can be seen to play a large part in Blanche's downfall.

A modern audience is perhaps able to see Blanche's plight more clearly. Society today is more prepared to concede to women some of the sexual freedoms that men have always enjoyed. Women at the time of the play, as defined by Mitch (a spokesman for his generation), were either good, marriageable women or prostitutes and 'not clean enough' (p.207). Blanche takes on the persona of whichever of these identities she needs at any time.

The statement suggests that Blanche may present a threat to the established order of the play's world. She is a single woman, 'an old maid' (p.150) and a dependent in-law in the Kowalski home, and her presence is unsettling to the comfortable arrangement of couples around her. Stanley cannot decide whether she is attractive and therefore available, as he believes any single woman must be, or off limits as his sister-in-law. In the world of the play, a woman achieves respectability and protection only when she is successful enough to win a husband. An un-partnered woman like Blanche has low status and is vulnerable to abuse.

By contrast, the play portrays the sexual freedoms men may enjoy without censure. Stanley, the soldiers and the men from the Hotel Flamingo express no remorse for their encounters with Blanche. The hypocritical social attitudes of the time ensure that Blanche must be punished for her indiscretions. Stanley's rape of his sister-in-law is violent, but even more cruel is his psychological destruction of a lonely, vulnerable woman.

Blanche's downfall is absolute by the end of the play. The hints of institutional brutality, such as the cutting of her nails and the use of a straitjacket as restraint, are horrifying reminders of the destiny in store for her. It is fitting that her journey will end in a government hospital as her transgressions have been against the conventions of her society.

QUESTIONS & ANSWERS

This section focuses on your own analytical writing on the text, and gives you strategies for producing high quality responses in your coursework and exam essays.

Essay writing – an overview

An essay is a formal and serious piece of writing that presents your point of view on the text, usually in response to a given essay topic. Your 'point of view' in an essay is your interpretation of the meaning of the text's language, structure, characters, situations and events, supported by detailed analysis of textual evidence.

Analyse – don't summarise

In your essays it is important to avoid simply summarising what happens in a text:

- A **summary** is a description or paraphrase (retelling in different words) of the characters and events. For example: 'Macbeth has a horrifying vision of a dagger dripping with blood before he goes to murder King Duncan'.
- An **analysis** is an explanation of the real meaning or significance that lies 'beneath' the text's words (and images, for a film). For example: 'Macbeth's vision of a bloody dagger shows how deeply uneasy he is about the violent act he is contemplating – as well as his sense that supernatural forces are impelling him to act'.

A limited amount of summary is sometimes necessary to let your reader know which part of the text you wish to discuss. However, always keep this to a minimum and follow it immediately with your analysis (explanation) of what this part of the text is really telling us.

Plan your essay

Carefully plan your essay so that you have a clear idea of what you are going to say. The plan ensures that your ideas flow logically, that your argument remains consistent and that you stay on the topic. An essay plan should be a list of **brief dot points** – no more than half a page. It includes:

- your central argument or main contention – a concise statement (usually in a single sentence) of your overall response to the topic. See 'Analysing a sample topic' for guidelines on how to formulate a main contention.
- three or four dot points for each paragraph indicating the main idea and evidence/examples from the text. Note that in your essay you will need to *expand* on these points and *analyse* the evidence.

Structure your essay

An essay is a complete, self-contained piece of writing. It has a clear beginning (the introduction), middle (several body paragraphs) and end (the last paragraph or conclusion). It must also have a central argument that runs throughout, linking each paragraph to form a coherent whole.

See examples of introductions and conclusions in the 'Analysing a sample topic' and 'Sample answer' sections.

The introduction establishes your overall response to the topic. It includes your main contention and outlines the main evidence you will refer to in the course of the essay. Write your introduction *after* you have done a plan and *before* you write the rest of the essay.

The body paragraphs argue your case – they present evidence from the text and explain how this evidence supports your argument. Each body paragraph needs:

- a strong **topic sentence** (usually the first sentence) that states the main point being made in the paragraph
- **evidence** from the text, including some brief quotations
- **analysis** of the textual evidence explaining its significance and **explanation** of how it supports your argument
- **links back to the topic** in one or more statements, usually towards the end of the paragraph.

Connect the body paragraphs so that your discussion flows smoothly. Use some linking words and phrases like 'similarly' and 'on the other hand', though don't start every paragraph like this. Another strategy is to use a significant word from the last sentence of one paragraph in the first sentence of the next.

Use key terms from the topic – or similes for them – throughout, so the relevance of your discussion to the topic is always clear.

The conclusion ties everything together and finishes the essay. It includes strong statements that emphasise your central argument and provide a clear response to the topic.

Avoid simply restating the points made earlier in the essay – this will end on a very flat note and imply that you have run out of ideas and vocabulary. The conclusion is meant to be a logical extension of what you have written, not just a repetition or summary of it. Writing an effective conclusion can be a challenge. Try using these tips:

- Start by linking back to the final sentence of the second-last paragraph – this helps your writing to 'flow', rather than just leaping back to your main contention straight away.
- Use similes and expressions with equivalent meanings to vary your vocabulary. This allows you to reinforce your line of argument without being repetitive.
- When planning your essay, think of one or two broad statements or observations about the text's wider meaning. These should be related to the topic and your overall argument. Keep them for the conclusion, since they will give you something 'new' to say but still follow logically from your discussion. The introduction will be focused on the topic, but the conclusion can present a wider view of the text.

Essay topics

1. 'In *A Streetcar Named Desire*, it is difficult to decide who deserves our sympathy more: Blanche or Stanley.' Discuss.
2. In Scene Ten, Stanley tells Blanche that they have "had this date ... from the beginning". Do you agree with him that his rape of Blanche was inevitable?
3. 'Despite his aggression and bravado, Stanley is shown to be a weak and insecure character.' Do you agree?
4. 'Both Blanche and Stella are victims of their own self-deception.' Do you agree?
5. 'Blanche is both a predator and a victim.' Discuss.
6. 'The central conflict in *A Streetcar Named Desire* is between the values of a decadent culture and those of the modern world.' Discuss.

7 '*A Streetcar Named Desire* presents the conflict between masculine and feminine ways of seeing the world.' Discuss.

8 '*A Streetcar Named Desire* demonstrates the powerful force of sexuality in human life.' Discuss.

9 '*A Streetcar Named Desire* reveals the tragedy of the social outcast who has nowhere to belong.' Discuss.

10 Blanche tells Mitch, "I'll tell you what I want. Magic!" How does the play portray the dangers of avoiding reality?

Vocabulary for writing on *A Streetcar Named Desire*

Ambivalence: having contradictory feelings towards a situation or character. The audience may be ambivalent about Stanley, sympathising with his annoyance towards Blanche but deploring his cruelty.

Catharsis: the cleansing feeling following the pity and terror that climax at the end of a tragedy. Blanche's fate at the end of the play can be cathartic for the audience.

Claustrophobia: dread of confined spaces. Blanche finds the little apartment claustrophobic and she feels trapped.

Conventional morality: socially accepted ways of behaving, especially sexually. Blanche outrages conventional morality in Laurel with her seduction of the student.

Facade: outward appearance, usually false or constructed. Blanche presents a facade of respectability.

Hubris: tragic pride that leads to a character's downfall. Blanche insists that she has a superior intellect and culture and this contributes to Stanley's determination to bring her down.

Irony: irony occurs when a meaning is intended that contradicts the literal meaning of the words. For example, 'Elysian Fields' is certainly no paradise, and Mitch is not the romantic hero that the name 'Rosenkavalier' suggests.

Neurosis: psychological illness, leading to behaviour characterised by abnormal insistence on unrealistic ideas. Blanche is neurotic in her constant lies and deceits.

Outcast, outsider: someone considered not fit to mix with society. Blanche becomes an outcast in Laurel.

Symbol: object, behaviour, action or image which represents something else (usually something less concrete) by association of ideas. The paper light shade symbolises Blanche's desire to cover up the ugliness of life. Her obsessive bathing is a symbol of her need to wash away guilt. The ride on the streetcars called Desire and Cemeteries symbolises the one-way journey towards death.

Tragedy: drama that depicts the suffering and downfall of the main character, or tragic hero, whose desire to achieve a goal is frustrated by a personal flaw. Blanche's search for peace is destroyed by her neurotic behaviour.

Analysing a sample topic

'Both Blanche and Stella are victims of their own self-deception.' Do you agree?

The topic seems straightforward but has some complexity. Although the question asks whether you agree with the statement, it is important not to merely list a number of examples of Blanche's and Stella's self-deceptions. It is also important to examine the characters separately. The topic asks not only if both women deceive themselves, but also whether this causes either or both of them to suffer, and to what degree. It may be that they are indeed victims, but of something other than self-deception.

You will need to consider what self-deception means. In what ways does Blanche delude herself? What is Stella not facing up to? Does the question imply that there may be something in their shared background which leads them to the same self-deceptive behaviour?

Deception means pretending to be what you are really not; self-deception means convincing yourself of this. You will need to decide whether the characters really believe in the truth of the way they project themselves. Does Blanche really believe she is the refined lady she claims to be? Is Stella really happy in her marriage to Stanley?

Introduction

Do you agree with the statement? Do you disagree with it? Or do you agree with part of it and partially disagree? Your introduction needs to state clearly which position you will take. This is the main contention, or main argument, of your response and you need to indicate the broad reasoning that your essay will follow. Here are some examples of main contentions:

Agreement: 'Both Blanche and Stella bring on their own suffering by being unwilling to face the truth of their situations.'

Disagreement: 'Although it is true that Blanche and Stella are victims in *A Streetcar Named Desire*, their suffering is due to the insensitivity and cruelty of other people.'

Partial agreement: 'Blanche's tragedy is caused by her inability to face the truth about herself, but Stella chooses to behave in her own best interests.'

The introduction also needs to indicate the main ideas you will use to support your contention.

Sample introduction

> Blanche's tragedy is caused by her inability to face the truth about herself, but Stella chooses to behave in her own best interests. Blanche's loathing for her past behaviour has driven her to delusions that verge on insanity. Stella, however, knows what her choices will cost and is motivated by selfishness, not self-deception. To some degree, both women are also victims of the conventional morality of the time.

Body paragraphs

Blanche is a victim, but not only of self-deception:

- Others judge her and society punishes her for her behaviour.
- 'This woman is morally unfit for her position!' (p.205).
- She is a victim of guilt – she blames herself for Allan's death.
- As she escapes into promiscuity she becomes a victim of self-deception.

Blanche's self-deception:

- She cannot accept her own sexuality.
- 'What you are talking about is brutal desire ...' (p.162).
- The deception leads to a fractured self-image – a discrepancy between her situation and her pride.

- 'The Hotel Flamingo is not the sort of establishment I would dare to be seen in!' (p.168).
- She is in denial about her fading beauty and her drinking addiction.

Stella is practical, a survivor:

- She chooses Stanley and life, over Belle Reve and death.
- 'The best I could do was make my own living ...' (p.126).
- She accepts Stanley's occasional violence as the price of a passionate relationship.
- She values 'things that happen between a man and a woman' (p.162).
- She suffers remorse at the play's end; she feels guilty, crying 'what have I done to my sister?' (p.224), but she knows what she has done and will continue to suffer for her betrayal.

Both women are victims of the strict gender roles of the time:

- Stella is prompted to choose Stanley over Blanche by the need to hang on to a male protector, a husband.
- 'I couldn't believe her story and go on living with Stanley' (p.217).
- Blanche is still looking for a man to rescue her at the end, still hoping for 'the kindness of strangers' (p.225).
- Blanche's desperate need for love has led her to delusion and breakdown.

Sample conclusion

> Both Stella and Blanche suffer from the prevailing moral attitudes of the time. Blanche is driven to keep up a facade of beauty and respectability in order to be acceptable to others and, tragically, to herself. It is a charade that drives her into insanity. Stella, too, feels the social imperative to hold on to her man and her marriage, at all costs. However, she is clear-eyed and pragmatic, choosing reluctantly to betray her sister and to experience the guilt that goes with such a choice.

SAMPLE ANSWER

'*A Streetcar Named Desire* reveals the tragedy of the social outcast who has nowhere to belong.' Discuss.

In Blanche DuBois, *A Streetcar Named Desire* presents a woman who is isolated, hounded and punished by society: a social outcast with nowhere to belong. The play shows her suffering to be much greater than her sins deserve, with total ostracism as her ultimate fate. Although the outcome for Blanche is not death, her psychological annihilation can be interpreted as a tragedy.

The play reveals the tenuous hold on security that human beings have. Blanche has enjoyed the protection of wealth and family standing, and the longed-for security of love and marriage, but when these are lost she spirals into poverty and a pattern of one-night stands. From her arrival at Elysian Fields, Blanche is seeking one last chance to find refuge, but her stiff manner and incongruous 'white suit with a fluffy bodice' mark her as out of place in a neighbourhood where people cling tenaciously to their friendships and their partners.

The play shows that such camaraderie is not available to the social outcast, whose place is to be homeless and despised. Blanche's position as an outsider is made clear by the fact that her presence is unwanted in the tiny apartment. She intrudes on the Kowalskis' lives and Stanley longs to 'get the coloured lights going with nobody's sister behind the curtain to hear us!' He barely tolerates Blanche from the beginning and is delighted to find evidence of her sexual misdemeanours to justify his torment and destruction.

Conventional morality is seen to be a cruel judge. In the 1940s world of the play, Blanche is exiled from Laurel for her promiscuity. Behaviour that may be acceptable for men like Kiefaber, Stanley and Shaw – who talk freely about their exploits at the Hotel Flamingo – is condemned in women. Although sex inside marriage was regarded as the social ideal, across all sections of society in the play, men, from travelling salesmen at the Hotel Flamingo to the wealthy landowners of Belle Reve, are seen to engage in 'epic fornications', and society turns a blind eye. Blanche is a victim of this hypocrisy.

The play reveals that homosexuality, too, was seen as flouting the social order, and, like female promiscuity, was unacceptable in society. Stella's derogatory euphemism for her brother-in-law is 'degenerate', implying that he is low and degraded. Allan had attempted to cover up his homosexuality by marrying Blanche in an effort to find a safe place in society, and when his sexual orientation became known, he saw no way out but suicide. The play evokes pity for both Allan and Blanche in their struggles to fit in, and leaves the audience to reflect on the cruel double standards that isolate and destroy them.

A Streetcar Named Desire shows that for outcasts, there is no way back into the social fold. Blanche pretends desperately to Mitch to be the virtuous woman he admires, telling him that 'a girl alone in the world' would be 'lost' if she gave in to her desires. Veering between the extremes of the femme fatale of the Hotel Flamingo, and the maidenly sister-in-law of Elysian Fields, Blanche is destabilised by her efforts to be what the men around her seem to want her to be. However, when her past sexual indiscretions come to light, there is no suggestion that forgiveness or fresh starts are options that will be offered to her. Stanley's threatening words – that her 'future is mapped out' – portend a grim fate for Blanche. In this society, a fallen woman is an outcast for life.

Blanche has missed her opportunity to find refuge and belonging. Her social isolation is partly due to her adherence to the manners and graces of a past culture. Unable to adapt to the modern world, she is ageing and fearful of becoming the 'old maid' she describes herself as to Mitch. A woman alone in a world where marriage and partnering are the norm is vulnerable. She has nowhere to belong because the world of her youth has passed. Blanche's efforts to secure a future with Mitch come too late and the play suggests that, in any case, such a mismatched relationship would not be the solution to Blanche's isolation.

The ultimate fate of the outcast is official exclusion from society. Blanche is cast into the hell of a mental institution as she becomes increasingly unable to function in a world that judges her as wicked and 'not clean enough to bring in the house'. Stanley's expressions of disapproval (which are backed up by Mitch) represent the common view.

Stanley is also the agent of a terrible physical assault on her, as if the judgement of society is that a promiscuous woman deserves nothing better than rape.

The play presents Blanche as a tragic victim of a strict social order and it invites the audience to be more critical of those who judge Blanche than of Blanche herself. Her deepest sorrow is the death of Allan rather than guilt at sleeping with the men of Laurel, and her sexual indiscretions are seen to be much less harmful than the relentless cruelty of those who bring her down.

REFERENCES & READING

Text

Williams, Tennessee 2000, *A Streetcar Named Desire and Other Plays*, Penguin, London.

Films

A Streetcar Named Desire 1951, dir. Elia Kazan, Warner Bros. Starring Vivien Leigh, Marlon Brando and Kim Hunter.

Gone with the Wind 1939, dir. Victor Fleming, Metro Goldwyn Mayer. Starring Vivien Leigh and Clark Gable.

Websites

Bak, John S. 2004, *Criticism on A Streetcar Named Desire: A Bibliographic Survey 1947–2003*, www.cercles.com/n10/bak.pdf

Farnsworth, Elizabeth 1997, *Fifty Years of Desire*, PBS, www.pbs.org/newshour/bb/entertainment/july-dec97/streetcar_11-11.html

Haley, Darryl E. 1999, *Certain Moral Values: A Rhetoric of Outcasts in the Plays of Tennessee Williams*, www.etsu.edu/haleyd/DissHome.html

Other references

Bailey, Jo 1993, 'Sexuality and *A Streetcar Named Desire*', in Caroline Gaylard, ed., *Players VCE Text Educational Package*, Monash University, Melbourne, pp.1–11.

Gilder, Rosamond 1948, 'The Playwright Takes Over', *Theatre Arts*, vol. 32, no. 1, pp.10–11.

Grove, Robin 1987, 'Being Taken for a Ride: *A Streetcar Named Desire*', in Brian McFarlane, ed., *Viewpoints 87*, Longman Cheshire, Melbourne, pp.217–22.

Krutch, Joseph Wood 1947, 'Drama', *The Nation*, vol. 165, pp.34–5.

Shaw, Irwin 1947, 'Masterpiece', *The New Republic*, vol. 17, pp.34–5.

Williams, Tennessee 1984, *A Streetcar Named Desire*, Methuen, London.

notes